THE
PURPOSE
PROJECT

a handbook for bringing meaning to life at work

CAROLYN TATE

This edition published by Carolyn Tate & Co Pty Ltd 2017

ISBN 978-0-646-97139-1

Disclaimer

Although the author and publisher have made every effort to ensure that the information in this book was correct at press time, the author and publisher do not assume and hereby disclaim any liability to any party for any loss, damage or disruption caused by errors or omissions, whether such errors or omissions result from negligence, accident or any other cause.

The material in this publication is of the nature of general comment only and does not represent professional advice. It is not intended to provide specific guidance for particular circumstances and it should not be relied on as the basis for any decision to take action or not take action on any matter which it covers. Readers should obtain professional advice where appropriate before making any decision. To the maximum extent permitted by the law, the author and publisher disclaim all responsibility and liability to any person, arising directly from any person taking or not taking action based on the information in this publication.

Book design by Irma Zimmermann of Tell IT Media.

Photography by Beth Jennings Photography.

For more information visit www.carolyntate.co

DEDICATION

To my son, Billy, a wholehearted young man who is living his life with passion and purpose to bring his true gifts to the world.

To my nephews Oscar, Archie, Sam, Henry and Louis and my niece Eve, may you go boldly forward to find that work that lights you up.

THE PURPOSE PROJECT

> *There's a crack, a crack in everything.*
> *That's how the light gets in.*
> - Leonard Cohen

There's more than a crack in the state of our world today. It's more like a chasm that's too wide to ignore. It's letting in a piercing light that's bringing humanity to a tipping point and it's heralding the dawn of a new age - *The Human Age* – the age where meaning is fast becoming the new money.

We're now asking ourselves life's most vital, yet deeply uncomfortable questions. What really matters to me beyond money and material goods? Am I achieving my highest potential? Am I doing work that is meaningful to me and in service to others? What's the contribution I have to make and the legacy I wish to leave?

In other words, what is my *why*? What is my purpose?

For many of us, doing work that fulfills our purpose seems like an impossibility. We've bought into the erroneous belief that we must flee our job (and life) to go in search of our *why* in some other job or company or as an entrepreneur.

The Purpose Project will bust that myth. It will help you unearth your purpose starting right where you are, right now, with all that you have, no matter where you work. Whether you're an employee, business owner or student, this book will help you turn your dreaming into doing through adopting your own *Purpose Project*.

> For many of us, doing work that fulfills our purpose seems like an impossibility. We've bought into the erroneous belief that we must flee our job (and life) to go in search of our *why* in some other job or company or as an entrepreneur.

The Purpose Project is also a handbook for the *Purpose Activists* in organisations – the ones who are passionate about balancing the imperative of profit with the imperative of purpose in order to create more humane workplaces.

It's time for us each to take responsibility for advancing *The Human Age* by bringing meaning to life at work.

If not you, who? If not now, when?

With love,

Carolyn

CONTENTS

About The Author ....*x*

Acknowledgements .... *xii*

INTRODUCTION 1

My Purpose Journey 3

Why We Need This Book 6

Who This Book Is For.. 9

How To Use This Book.................................... 13

PART 1: GETTING STARTED ON PURPOSE...................................**19**

What is Purpose?... 21

The History of Purpose (lessness)................... 27

The Future of Purpose..................................... 31

Purpose Drives Prosperity 35

Robert's Story 38

The Purpose Project 40

Setting Your Intention 43

PART 2: DISCOVERING YOUR PERSONAL WORK PURPOSE................. **49**

Finding Your Work Purpose.............................. 51

Discover Your *Ikigai* 54

Laura's Story.. 59

Your 50 Purpose Questions.............................. 61

Start Where You Are 68

Karen's Story 70

The Signs of Purpose 72

Become a Purpose Activist 74

PART 3: UNEARTHING THE PURPOSE OF YOUR ORGANISATION 75

The Purpose of Your Enterprise 77

The Prosperity-Driven Enterprise 81

Purpose. Vision. Mission. Values. 85

The 3 Levels of Purpose 90

The (Higher) Purpose Statement 95

SafetyCulture's Story 100

Telstra's Story 102

The Purpose Health-Check 104

The Purpose Effect 107

The Manifesto 109

It's Up to You 112

PART 4: THE 12 PRACTICES OF PURPOSE 115

Introducing the 12 Practices 117

Practice 1: The Practice of Surrendering 119

Practice 2: The Practice of Finding Courage 125

Practice 3: The Practice of Self-Care 131

Practice 4: The Practice of Re-Learning 138

Practice 5: The Practice of Becoming Conscious 144

Practice 6: The Practice of Redefining Success 151

Practice 7: The Practice of Curiosity 158

Practice 8: The Practice of Creativity 165

Practice 9: The Practice of Love & Compassion 171

Practice 10: The Practice of Embracing Nature 178

Practice 11: The Practice of Being In Community 185

Practice 12: The Practice of Living Simply 192

Reviewing your Practices 198

PART 5: CREATING YOUR PURPOSE PROJECT **201**

Why Purpose Projects? 203

Scoping your Purpose Project... 206

Conclusion 209

Index 213

Connect with Carolyn *220*

Other Books by Carolyn.. *221*

ABOUT THE AUTHOR

In 2010, after a long career in marketing in the corporate world and in her own marketing consultancy, Carolyn left her home in Sydney, Australia to take a career circuit-breaker in the south of France with her son, Billy.

In 2011 she returned to live in Melbourne and went to work at a women's not-for-profit before founding Carolyn Tate & Co., an education and publishing company dedicated to unearthing a higher purpose in people and organisations.

Carolyn is a keynote speaker and the founder of *The Purpose Project* and *Talk on Purpose* learning programs and *The Slow School of Business* (*Slow School*)*. She's a founding member of *Conscious Capitalism Australia* (a movement that exists to inspire businesses to a purpose beyond profit) and her company is also a *Certified B Corporation* (this is like the Fairtrade Coffee certification but for business).

She has been immersing herself in the concepts around higher purpose and the principles of consciousness in business for the past seven years and has been actively working with the contents of this book in her own personal and professional life and with clients.

Carolyn is also the author of *Small Business Big Brand* (2007), *Marketing your Small Business for Dummies* (2010), *Unstuck in Provence* (2014) and *Conscious Marketing* (2015). She's been a professional speaker for many years and has featured in the AFR, BRW, Herald-Sun, The Age, Peppermint Magazine and Slow Living.

 Watch Carolyn Tate's talk on The Slow School of Business YouTube channel.

In a world where fast-change, quick-profit and short-term thinking dominates, we believe the principles of the 'slow movement' should be applied to business and learning.

*What is *Slow School* you might be asking? We're a people-powered learning community dedicated to building purpose-driven and prosperous businesses that make the world a better place. Why "slow"? In a world where fast-change, quick-profit and short-term thinking dominates, we believe the principles of the 'slow movement' should be applied to business and learning. It's an ideology which espouses that fast is not better, and that a conscious and mindful approach often yields faster, more fruitful results.

ACKNOWLEDGEMENTS

The inspiration for *The Purpose Project* has come from the hundreds of business leaders I've interviewed, studied, coached and supported over my 30+ year working life.

The backbone of the book, however, is made up of my purpose-driven co-conspirators at *Slow School*, those of you who've supported me through 'thick and thin' in bringing this purpose work to life. There are too many to mention here but you know who you are. You have my deepest love and appreciation for your belief in me and the purpose work.

Thank you also to the many people who've found the courage to share your story at our *Talk on Purpose* courses. I applaud each of you for stepping forward and providing me with the real-life stories that give this book meaning and credibility.

While the writing of this book has been a solo pursuit, giving birth to it has been a most wonderful collaboration of hearts, heads and hands. Thank you to Irma Zimmermann for the exquisite creative design, Beth Jennings for the amazing photography, Marlene Rattigan for your dynamic editing and Billy Stafford for your digital prowess.

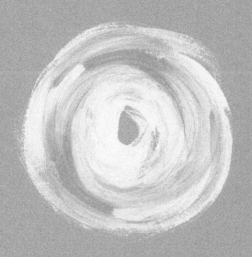

INTRODUCTION

MY PURPOSE JOURNEY

> *Writing is the only thing that, when I do it, I don't feel I should be doing something else.*
> - Gloria Steinem

I truly am at my happiest when writing. I never feel like I should be doing something else. Distractions are rare and I almost always achieve my daily word count.

That doesn't mean the words are always perfect. Often they're pretty tragic, I suspect. Funnily enough, it simply doesn't matter to me. My job is just to do the work, to get up every day and write like no one will ever read my words and then worry about them later.

My job is to take action to fulfil my highest purpose of writing books that truly matter.

That's what happens when you're 'on purpose' and doing work you love. The absolute priority is to get the job done, to strive for completion not perfection.

But, it's been a long and often arduous journey to get to this point.

In 2010, after a 20-year marketing career in the corporate world and in my own business, I came to the great realisation that I no longer had a passion for my profession.

So just like that, I gave it all up. I sold my home, gave away all my possessions, closed my business and went to live in beautiful Aix-en-Provence in the south of France with my son Billy, who was 12 at the time.

For six glorious months, while Billy went to the International Bilingual School of Provence, I set about recovering my health and wellbeing and rediscovering my spirituality and creativity.

This time in France was a pivotal point in my life. Mostly because it was the first time I'd ever taken time out to deeply question my raison d'être particularly with regard to my future livelihood. It was a time of deep, and at times, uncomfortable contemplation.

My work story is not unlike millions of other people's stories. Like many of us, I'd 'fallen into' my career without ever consciously choosing it.

In 1980, at the age of 18, I was living in Mt Gambier in rural South Australia. Despite an inner calling to become a teacher, I joined the local branch of the Commercial Bank of Australia, soon to become Westpac. In reality, it was the money that lured me there and the promise of promotion and prosperity that kept me there – not an excitement for the world of finance.

It was, however, an incredible learning ground, giving me the opportunity to fulfil a whole range of roles in branch banking, sales, training and finally marketing around 1990 which led to marketing management roles in Papua New Guinea and Westpac's Olympic sponsorship.

After 17 years at Westpac, I went to work with the investment bank Merrill Lynch as a marketing manager. It seemed that I was destined to have a lifelong career as a marketer.

Then not long after, in 2001 my life took a drastic about-turn. My marriage ended, Billy and I moved house and I quit my job to become a business owner. I chose to transfer my corporate marketing skills into my own business as a marketing consultant and teacher.

Still, I didn't question whether marketing was 'the thing' I was being called to do. It took me nine years of working in my own marketing business before it finally hit me in 2010 that I'd lost all enthusiasm for the profession.

This painful realisation was one of the catalysts for a radical decision to give everything up and start over again – in France. (A course of action that I don't necessarily recommend by the way, and one of the reasons for this book.)

In France, where we knew no one and couldn't speak the language, I was forced to be open to everything and attached to nothing. I embraced being in the present and going with the flow. I was free to be me – and write.

With the support of *The Artist's Way* (a book by Julia Cameron designed to help you discover your creative self), my trusty computer and an open heart, I set about writing the manuscript for *Unstuck in Provence*, all while exploring the wonders of Provence. It was one of the most delicious highlights of my life.

On our return to live in Melbourne in 2011, I took on a whole series of projects (aka experiments) to gain the clarity I was seeking. I went to work for a women's not-for-profit called *Fitted for Work*, started my education and publishing company *Carolyn Tate & Co.*, published *Unstuck in Provence* and *Conscious Marketing* and founded *The Slow School of Business*, our *Talk on Purpose* course and now *The Purpose Project*.

And I haven't even begun to list the projects that are no longer in existence (note how I carefully avoided the word 'failed'). Each project, whether alive and kicking today, or not, has helped me fine-tune my future work direction and has been an incredible learning experience. I've come to understand inherently, that we learn best by doing and testing.

As Oscar Wilde said, "the riskiest thing in life is taking no risks at all".

It's now seven years since I found the courage to move to France, start over and step onto the path to purpose. For me, it was a risk worth taking because it ultimately led me to writing this book for you.

I hope *The Purpose Project* becomes a book that truly matters to you and that it helps guide you towards a more meaningful work life.

WHY WE NEED THIS BOOK

> *You never change things by fighting the existing reality. To change something, build a new model that makes the existing model obsolete.*
> - Buckminster Fuller

On the 21st January 2017, nearly five million people marched in 500 cities, in 80 countries across the world at the *Women's March*. From Washington to the Antarctic to Melbourne – women, men and children gathered and made a stand for human rights, women's rights, LGBTQI rights and the rights of Mother Earth.

The inauguration of the 45th President of the USA held the mirror up to humanity, turning millions and millions of people from apathy to activism in one giant global gathering. It was the wake-up call the world desperately needed. This event started the mass movement away from our dominant world-state of separation and destruction towards co-operation and reparation and towards the pursuit of something far greater than power and profit.

It was the catalyst for the dawning of a new age – *The Human Age* – the age where finding meaning and making a difference, matters most.

So, now we find ourselves facing two choices. We can choose to ignore the new age on our doorstep and return to our apathy or we can choose the more courageous path and turn to greater activism, not in a placard-carrying, street-marching kind of way, but in daily activism in the way we live and work.

We simply can't leave it to the appointed leaders of our institutions and our governments to build the new systems required to make change happen.

It's not their responsibility alone to lead this 21st century reformation. It's up to each of us to take radical responsibility for this change, starting in our own backyard – because the state of the world starts with us.

It starts by digging deep into our own inner world so we can create change in our outer world. And we don't all have to run away from our current work and life either. We can explore the full possibility and potential to bring more meaning to our work, starting right where we are.

Khalil Gibran, the American artist, poet and writer said, "when you are born, your work is placed in your heart". I do believe this is true. We were born with a calling to do great work and make a difference, but after years of industrialisation and indoctrination, it's been repressed and we've been diverted away from realising our true gifts. We haven't unearthed what we're here to create, so we end up doing work that depletes us instead of completes us.

This is supported by the findings of a 2012 global Gallup poll that shows a mere 13% of employees are actively engaged at work, while 87% are either not engaged or actively disengaged. It would seem that 87% of the world's workers are making a 'dying' instead of a 'living' at work. How do we bring life back to work? How do we turn this tragic statistic around?

I believe the answer lies in radically reorienting people and the organisations they work for towards a higher purpose than profit.

And we do this by digging deep into our passions, talents and strengths and by exploring those gifts we have to offer and those things we want to fix in the world. We do this at both a personal and organisational level. We do it by addressing both our personal and collective pain, because pain always leads to finding purpose.

Deep down we all want to find our *why* in the workplace. We all want to do work that lights us up, that makes a difference and that creates prosperity as a result. That's why we

> We were born with a calling to do great work and make a difference, but after years of industrialisation and indoctrination, it's been repressed and we've been diverted away from realising our true gifts. We haven't unearthed what we're here to create, so we end up doing work that depletes us instead of completes us.

need *The Purpose Project*, a handbook and course that's designed for the humanists in the world.

Imagine for a moment, a world where everyone wakes up inspired to be going to work, just knowing the work we're doing is in service to our soul and in service to the souls of others. Just imagine!

Of one thing, you can be certain. The world needs you. Humanity needs you. Mother Earth needs you. We need millions and millions of passionate, purpose-driven people like you to keep the light shining bright and to make shift happen.

WHO THIS BOOK IS FOR

> *When the student is ready, the teacher will appear. When the student is truly ready... the teacher will disappear.*
> - Lao Tzu

If you believe in the status quo of our current world and that we simply have to accept things as they are, then this book is not for you. If you believe that it's not your responsibility to make change happen and you don't have any power to make change happen, then this book is not for you.

This book is for you, if you believe it's possible to do work that is meaningful to you, that makes a positive contribution to the world. This book is for you if you are ready, willing and able to shake things up, to get out of the conditioned patterns of the past and to take action.

This book is for the appointed leaders of big companies dedicated to bringing a higher purpose to their companies and everyone who works with them. It's for the self-leaders, irrespective of job title, who are brave enough to champion a higher purpose in the workplace. It's for entrepreneurs riding the highs and lows of the start-up world and business owners who have already had success but just know there's something far greater they'd like to contribute to the world.

It's for school students and university students willing to go outside the confines of conventional education and traditional employment paths in search of their calling. It's for school counsellors and parents charged with the responsibility of guiding the careers of our youth. It's for couples and families who wish to support each other to be their best.

It's for anyone in transition towards a new work life: students finishing high-school, mothers and fathers becoming empty-nesters, people approaching retirement, being made redundant or undergoing a career change.

A NOTE FOR BUSINESS LEADERS & EMPLOYEES

There's a growing body of evidence and research proving that the balance between purpose and profit is now both imperative and urgent.

In a recent survey titled *The Business Case for Purpose,* a team from Harvard Business Review and Ernst & Young's Beacon Institute declared "a new leading edge: those companies able to harness the power of purpose to drive performance and profitability will enjoy a distinct competitive advantage".

Billions of dollars each year are being spent on change and culture programs in companies, while it's claimed that over 70% of them are deemed to be failures. Programs centred on the fundamental underlying *why* of what you do are the ones that elicit intrinsic motivation from your people and that have most chance of succeeding.

There's also a proliferation of wannabe and recent 'corporate escapees' in the world. They're experienced people with great skills and talents who are committed to personal growth and reaching their full potential. They're feeling increasingly 'out of alignment' with the organisation's culture and desperately want to bring more meaning to their workplace. These are the people at most risk of leaving, and the very ones that companies most need to keep. And then there's the Millennials. They too, wish to only work for purpose-driven companies.

The key to purpose success in organisations lies in finding these people, the self-leaders – the *Purpose Activists*, and through empowering them to bring purpose to life through *Purpose Projects*. This handbook offers the tools, models and practices

In a recent survey titled *The Business Case for Purpose,* a team from Harvard Business Review and Ernst & Young's Beacon Institute declared "a new leading edge: those companies able to harness the power of purpose to drive performance and profitability will enjoy a distinct competitive advantage".

required for this. That's why I recommend giving a copy of this book to all your people and deeply engaging them in the course.

A NOTE FOR ENTREPRENEURS, START-UPS & SMALL BUSINESS OWNERS

Starting and growing a flourishing business is the toughest gig in town. The long hours and the slim chances of real success, require incredible faith, resilience and persistence. Without a *why* beyond making money, you may not have the fortitude required to 'keep on keeping on' when the going gets tough.

Your purpose, clearly articulated and communicated well, is the very thing that will attract the best partners, suppliers, investors, customers and employees to help you grow your business in the right direction. It will become the thing to guide you through the tough decisions and the driver of your business strategy. It will become the centre of your branding, marketing, sales, recruitment strategies and so much more.

If you've created a business that needs a greater dose of purpose to balance the drive for profit, this book is for you and your team too. Use the tools and practices to deeply explore your purpose. Invite all the people essential to the success of your business to get involved, including your life partner and family members. Not only will your business benefit from doing this work, but everyone will benefit personally too.

A NOTE FOR STUDENTS, EDUCATORS AND PARENTS

Our education system is currently facing incredible challenges and opportunities. It needs to change in order to equip youth with the skills required to live a globally connected, increasingly automated and nomadic work life, while still giving them a sense of stability and belonging in our uncertain world.

As adults, we must guide our youth to unearth their passions not only through their formal education but through self-directed learning outside of school and through a learn-by-doing approach. Through experimentation and project-based activities that tap into their creativity and curiosity, students will start to discover their potential vocation/s.

It's my aim for *The Purpose Project* to become required reading for secondary school students and the basis of a course for students navigating their way through choosing subjects, university courses and jobs.

A NOTE FOR COUPLES AND FAMILIES

The Purpose Project is also a practical guide to creating harmonious and happy partnerships, families and households.

A successful and enduring partnership is actually a spiritual practice, one where two fully aware human beings, both healthy and functional in their own right, come together to create something greater. A relationship built on consciousness, mutual understanding and a shared vision, also offers autonomy for each individual to pursue their own passions.

Sadly, many relationships become so familiar over time that each partner ends up estranged from the other. There is little deep intimacy or vulnerability which results in two people not really, truly knowing each other and, therefore, being unable to 'show up' in support of the other's dreams.

As adults, we must guide our youth to unearth their passions not only through their formal education but through self-directed learning outside of school and through a learn-by-doing approach. Through experimentation and project-based activities that tap into their creativity and curiosity, students will start to discover their potential vocation/s.

My greatest wish is for partners and families to delve into this handbook together as a conduit to strengthening family bonds through the adoption of both collective and personal pet projects.

HOW TO USE THIS BOOK

A HANDBOOK AND A COURSE

Think of this handbook as a course where each of the five parts builds upon the other culminating in the completion of an assignment – your *Purpose Project*.

Part 1 – Getting Started on Purpose

This section is devoted to putting some context around purpose in the workplace and why it's an imperative today. You will also set your intention for working with this course.

Part 2 – Discovering Your Personal Work Purpose

In this part you'll explore your own personal *why* in terms of your livelihood working with the purpose 'ikigai' model and accompanying activities.

Part 3 – Unearthing the Purpose of Your Organisation

Part 3 is focused on unearthing organisational purpose and bringing it to life. While it's more focused on the world of business, it's still highly relevant for any collective beyond the individual (communities, charities and teams).

Part 4 – The 12 Practices of Purpose

This part has a different flavour altogether from the others. We delve more deeply into 12 practices to support you in gaining clarity and I share the stories of people who are on the path.

Part 5 – Your Purpose Project

Part 5 is where you discover what constitutes a great *Purpose Project* and how to create the outline of your own project to get you started on the right path.

Part 1 is essential as it gives you the context required for the course. You can then change the order in which you work on parts 2, 3 and 4 although it does work best sequentially. Part 5, the part where you set your project is, of course, the ultimate aim of this book!

You may choose to read the book through in its entirety first without doing any exercises, while highlighting pertinent points as you go. You can then go back and work your way through the activities in a way that suits you.

TAKING AN ACTIVE APPROACH

Please don't just read this book. Live it, breathe it, write in it and most of all, take action with it. Action always precedes clarity and we learn best through 'inspiraction' (yes, I made this word up).

Inspiraction [noun]: An emotionally and/or spiritually inspired idea that compels one to take action without delay. Otherwise known as 'inspired action'.

Throughout the course you will need to take time out for various personal and/or group work. This icon indicates where action is required.

Research: At times, I recommend you undertake your own research such as reading other articles or books or studying other people, organisations or issues to inform your own approach and generate ideas.

Group work: If you're working in a company or in teams, there are a number of activities you can lead with your peers. Before undertaking these activities, it would be useful for others to have read this book too.

Reflection and/or meditation: Taking the time to go inward, to meditate and reflect on the questions throughout this book, is an essential practice in helping you focus your attention and intention.

Inspiration [noun]: An emotionally and/or spiritually inspired idea that compels one to take action without delay. Otherwise known as 'inspired action'.

Journaling exercises: Journaling is essential to the success of this course and it's a great way for you to gain clarity of thought and arrive at the answers to your most vital questions. (See more on journaling below).

Daily practices: Habits that do not serve us can be hard to kick but they limit our capacity to reach our potential. You'll be asked to assess some of these habits and adopt small daily changes and improvements.

Big action: Often we need to do something more significant to affect change that will take us far outside our comfort zone (and keep us there). You'll be required to do one daring thing each week to advance you towards your calling.

YouTube talks: The book features the stories of a number of people who've completed the *Talk on Purpose* course. Watch their 3-minute talks on *The Slow School of Business* YouTube channel.

THE POWER OF JOURNALING

Journaling is the primary key to the success of this course. Your journal is the place to record your ideas, promises and commitments to action and it enables you to see just how far you've come as you progress through the course.

I personally love the feel of pen on paper and prefer it to online journaling, particularly as I spend so much time on my computer writing books and blogs. I also like the fact that I can't edit or correct my writing as I believe every word serves a purpose.

If you choose to use a paper journal, you can buy a gorgeous journal or a simple A4 spiral note book with at least 200+ lined pages in it (which is actually more practical and pliable in my experience). In addition to writing in it, you can stick in images that are meaningful to you. It's also helpful to have coloured pens and stick-it notes on hand for highlighting your big revelations and ideas.

If you prefer to use an online journal, check out Evernote or 750 Words. There's no right or wrong way to get your words out, you just need to get them out using the tool that works best for you.

Please note that you don't need to be a 'writer' to journal. All you need is your journal, a pen and some dedicated private time. You also need to let go of some of the judgments that will come up. "But I can't write." "It feels childish." "I have nothing worth writing about." "It seems so self-indulgent and self-centred." These are all things you might tell yourself when you first start. Do it anyway! After a few weeks, it will become second nature and you'll start to look forward to it. Make journaling a habit, just like brushing your teeth.

As mentioned, there are designated exercises for you to journal on in the book; however, you may read a specific sentence, quote or story that particularly resonates for you. I'd also suggest journaling on what they invoke in you and why.

SETTING UP THE FOUNDATIONS

To do this work (and yourself) justice, you will need to set up a routine to complete the course. You might read a certain number of pages and then do one activity per day for the first hour of each morning or you may set aside four hours every Sunday afternoon to work on it.

Only you know your life and the other commitments you have to your family, work, hobbies and friends. Whatever you do though, please, please, please establish a routine and, therefore, the self-discipline to consistently do the work. Block out time in your diary and treat it like you would any other important appointment. Also, I'd much rather see you do it slowly and mindfully over 12 months than start at break-neck speed and give up after a month. Consistency and persistency are the key to long lasting change.

Your routine may include working with a 'purpose buddy' or a mastermind group on a weekly or monthly basis to review past achievements, future promises or even to form project teams. This group may consist of your co-workers, your family, your friends or a group of business owners.

Jim Rohn once famously said, "you are the average of the five people you spend the most time with". This is a sound warning to carefully choose the people you invite into this group. Look for the qualities you most admire and desire that will be helpful to you and the whole group.

This work can be mentally and emotionally challenging. It may bring up fear, resistance, old wounds, judgment (towards me, yourself and others) and feelings of helplessness. Stick with it. If you need support, get it. This support may come from a qualified therapist, your purpose buddy, a trusted mentor or a well-qualified friend, and most likely a combination of these.

On the flip-side, be mindful who you share this work with outside your support team. The ones closest to you, friends and family members (unless they're doing this course with you), while well-meaning, may unknowingly railroad your efforts through their negativity or unsolicited advice. Your life must be treated as your own private work of art. Take care to protect yourself and surround yourself with the right people and the right circumstances to thrive.

Also, while doing this work, you'll need to look after your physical health and wellbeing. Without a good diet, plenty of sleep, regular exercise, lots of water and the limiting (or elimination) of harmful substances such as smoking, alcohol or fatty foods, you'll not have the mental acuity to make good choices and take sound action. Health first, everything else second!

Ready? Let's get started!

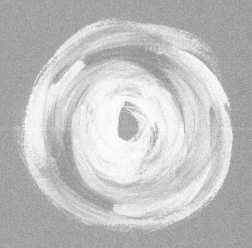

PART 1

GETTING STARTED ON PURPOSE

WHAT IS PURPOSE?

> *The two most important days of your life are the day you are born and the day you find out why.*
> - Mark Twain

The importance of living and working 'on purpose' has been the subject of many a philosopher, artist, writer and spiritual leader.

Joseph Campbell said, "follow your bliss". Pablo Picasso said, "the meaning of life is to find your gift. The purpose of life is to give it away".

And now even business leaders are weighing in on the subject. Richard Branson once claimed, "explore this next great frontier where the boundaries between work and higher purpose are merging into one, where doing good, really is good for business".

But what is this thing called 'purpose'? What does it actually mean in terms of your work and the organisation you own, lead or work for?

No doubt you have a million questions.

At a personal level, you may be pondering on these questions. Where can purpose be found and where do I start looking for it? Can I make a living from it? Do I have just one purpose or are there multiple possibilities? Do I have to leave my current job to find it or can I find it where I am now? How do I know if I have found my purpose?

At an organisational level, you may also be asking many questions. How do we create a company purpose that is meaningful and actionable?

But what is this thing called 'purpose'? What does it actually mean in terms of your work and the organisation you own, lead or work for?

How do we balance the imperative of profit with a higher purpose? How do I connect our people to the collective purpose? How will a higher purpose improve productivity and employee happiness?

These are all valid and meaningful questions that you'll be guided to answer for yourself throughout this book.

DEFINING PURPOSE

Purpose is all about living and working at the intersection of your talents and passion in service to yourself and the greater good. It's about living a life and doing work that serves you, humanity and the planet. It's about feeling content in the knowing that what you're doing makes you feel more human, more alive and more valuable.

It answers the fundamental questions: what really matters to me beyond money and material goods; what do I stand for and believe in; what is the contribution I have to make; how is the world better because I exist; what is the legacy I wish to leave?

In other words, why am I here? What is my *why* – my purpose?

It's vital right now that I ground the concept of purpose into something tangible, actionable and practical lest it be seen as something too lofty and unattainable.

Purpose is a stable and generalized intention to accomplish something that is at the same time meaningful to the self [organisation] and consequential for the world beyond the self [organisation].
- William Damon, Path to Purpose

Purpose is a stable and generalized intention to accomplish something that is at the same time meaningful to the self [organisation] and consequential for the world beyond the self [organisation].

- William Damon, Path to Purpose

This definition works at both a personal and organisational level. I've inserted the words 'organisation' next to the word 'self'. An 'organisation' is any entity created outside an individual that becomes a collective of two or more people: a small business, a major corporation, a government body, an industry association, a not-for-profit or charity, a community, a school, a sports team and even a couple or family.

There are three essential elements to this definition. Firstly, that there's an intention to 'accomplish something', a path to take, a goal to achieve or a project to undertake. Secondly, it must be 'meaningful' to us which means we're passionate about it and it enables us to reach our highest potential while making the most of our skills and talents. Thirdly, it's 'consequential for the world' which means that it's in service to others and that it makes a difference.

The first part of this definition around the notion of having to 'accomplish something' is why this book has been named *The Purpose Project*. Your purpose arrives through doing and achieving something, not by just thinking about it, which is where most of us remain stuck.

THE FLUIDITY OF PURPOSE

Through the course of writing this book, I've come to understand that purpose is not a solid, set and forget, single-minded notion for each person. We must take the heat off ourselves to find 'that one thing' that will keep our motor running forever. It's a myth, and I would be doing you grievous harm if you were to believe there was only one guiding north-star for you.

At a personal level, we each have many things that are truly meaningful to us that will result in various projects and accomplishments. While in this book we focus on work purpose, the principles can apply to any area of our life. Also, even in our work, we can each have multiple purposes that will change over time as we learn and grow and our values and beliefs change. For example, my highest personal work purpose and the one that will never die, is: "to write books that truly matter", while the purpose of my company and this book is: "to unearth a higher purpose in people and organisations". This second purpose will most definitely change for me in years to come once I'm certain I've left the legacy for others to carry it on.

> Your purpose arrives through doing and achieving something, not by just thinking about it, which is where most of us remain stuck.

Also, as the famous song *Beautiful Boy* by John Lennon goes, "life is what happens to us while we are making other plans". Sometimes our best laid purpose plans can turn on a pin-head due to good fortune or misfortune and we get called towards a new even higher purpose that we may never have conceived possible. While we must remain steadfastly focused on working towards our purpose, we must also remain unattached and open to the beautiful, wild, universal possibilities.

While a human may have multiple purposes, at an enterprise level, there must only be one clear *why* in order to galvanise effective action – like bees in a hive all working towards the single-minded purpose of making sweet, sweet honey.

DEFINING 'HIGHER PURPOSE'

You'll notice throughout this book that I often use the words 'higher purpose'. There are three reasons for this.

Firstly, a higher purpose is like a higher power, it's something outside of us that intrinsically drives us. While we must still do the work, we're also being guided by something bigger than ourselves – call it the universe, spirit, God, nature or whatever else works for you. When you have a clear intention towards fulfilling your purpose (and if you are paying attention), you'll notice that the very people, opportunities and circumstances that you most need, will present themselves. Synchronicity is at play and magic happens.

Secondly, the higher purpose implies that it's about being 'in service' to something beyond the individual and the organisation itself. It's ultimately in service to all of your stakeholders not just those who transact with you (employees, customers and suppliers) but the community in which you operate, society, humankind and the environment. We exist in a delicate eco-system and our choices will have consequences (intended or unintended) that will either negatively or positively impact this eco-system.

> Sometimes our best laid purpose plans can turn on a pin-head due to good fortune or misfortune and we get called towards a new even higher purpose that we may never have conceived possible.

Thirdly, higher purpose implies that it's noble, just, moral and ethical – not necessarily legal. There are many activities occurring in this world that happen to be legal, which are unjust. There are also many activities one would deem to be just, that are actually illegal.

Higher purpose is, of course, a highly subjective notion. What I believe to be the truth and to be ethical and moral will most definitely be different to your beliefs. Just be prepared to question the notion of higher purpose as you work through this book. We'll be exploring your truth and what you stand for as the foundation of your purpose-driven work.

ANOTHER WORD FOR PURPOSE

It seems that 'purpose' is the word on everyone's lips right now. There's a plethora of new books, journals, TED talks and articles being released on the topic since Simon Sinek brought it to the mainstream arena in his *Start with Why* book and TED talk. Even Justin Bieber has weighed in on the subject with his 'Purpose' song, album and world tour.

I have a bit of a love/hate relationship with the word as I believe many people and organisations are both misunderstanding and mistreating it. It's seen as a trend and something for the marketing or PR department to play with as more of an advertising line rather than the catalyst for affecting deep change in the workplace.

So, if you would like to opt for a different word, feel free to replace it with any of the following: mission, passion, meaning, calling, cause, reason for being, ikigai (the Japanese term for 'reason for being'), intention, livelihood, your *why*, true north, vocation, highest potential and finally my personal favourite; 'raison d'être' (the French phrase for 'reason for being').

Throughout the book, I'll deliberately switch between these different terms for purpose so that we don't get hung up on the word. In reality, however, it has nothing to do with the words we use. What really matters is your intention and then the action you take. Actions speak far louder than words!

Set a timer for 30 minutes and write as much as you can on the following questions.

Why are you doing this course?

What are all the questions you have about purpose?

What are you feeling sceptical about and why?

What are you feeling hopeful about and why?

THE HISTORY OF PURPOSE (LESSNESS)

Challenging the meaning of life is the truest expression of the state of being human.

- Victor Frankl

Psychotherapist, Victor Frankl, wrote the seminal book on purpose called *Man's Search for Meaning*. At the time of Frankl's death in 1997, the book had sold over 10 million copies and it had been translated into 24 languages.

The book is a chronicle of his tragic experiences in an Auschwitz concentration camp during World War II. According to Frankl, the way a prisoner imagined his life outside the camp affected his longevity. In the book, he put forward a theory on a form of psychotherapy called logo-therapy which he used to make sense of his own experience and that of his fellow prisoners.

Unlike psycho-analysis which tends to focus on the past, logo-therapy confronts patients with, and reorients them towards the meaning of their life. Logo-therapy derives from the word 'logos', the Greek word for meaning. Frankl argues in the book that our search for meaning is our primary motivation in life and that this meaning is unique and specific and can only be fulfilled by the person alone. He asserts that through finding a higher purpose and a deeper meaning, people are capable of enduring even the worst atrocities.

Frankl's meaning in life became to help others find theirs.

Out of the concentration camp, Frankl conducted research with students at the Johns Hopkins University. He examined nearly 8000 students from around 48 colleges, asking them what was most important to them on leaving university: 16% said it was 'making lots of money', while 78% said it was 'finding purpose and meaning'.

So, what does this research tell us? It tells us that deep down we are hardwired to seek a life (and livelihood) that has purpose and meaning.

If purpose and meaning are so important, how is it that so many of us have not pursued it?

THE INDUSTRIAL AGE KILLED PURPOSE

In part, I blame the industrial age for killing higher purpose in humankind.

Man's Search for Meaning was published in 1946 after WWII ended. The post-war period took industrialisation to a whole new level and the age was evermore defined by the factory, the assembly line and mass production.

While this period brought on many great advancements for humanity, it also created an economic system that turned us all simultaneously (and mindlessly) into consumers and workers. The more we consumed, the more we needed to earn and the more we needed to work. And a vicious cycle of consumption, having stuff and having more, became our default measure of success. The measure of a country's well-being became all about GDP (Gross Domestic Product) not about the health and happiness of the nation's people. Compare this to the country of Bhutan whose primary measure of success is GNH (Gross National Happiness).

The economic system was built on the mass production of products where demand for these products was fuelled by mass promotion and where profit was the single-minded goal. There was no higher purpose than profit while people and our planet earth became commoditised and dispensable.

> The measure of a country's well-being became all about GDP (Gross Domestic Product) not about the health and happiness of the nation's people. Compare this to the country of Bhutan whose primary measure of success is GNH (Gross National Happiness).

Money and material possessions became the meaning of life in the industrial era and we were all just so busy consuming and working that we didn't stop to think about what would really bring us joy and fulfil our potential.

PARENTS & THE EDUCATION SYSTEM KILLED PURPOSE

We were also cheated out of discovering our purpose by parents and an education system built to provide the human capital required to meet the demands of the industrialised world.

As we grew up, many of us were told by parents and teachers to make our passion (if we even had one) our hobby instead of our livelihood. For many of us, our true creative potential was never unleashed. It was repressed instead of expressed and at best, tolerated. We were advised to follow a more practical path, one that would be sure to result in a steady job with a regular income or a professional career that would maximise our wealth and societal standing.

Many of us were also being channelled into pursuing noble family vocations. The farmer's son became a farmer. The doctor's daughter became a doctor. The king's son became a king. We were unconsciously (and consciously in many cases) being groomed for our career by our ancestors from birth.

We were also forced from a very early age to start planning our lives: to choose schools, to choose subjects, to choose universities, to choose careers, to choose partners, to choose marriage, to choose having kids. We were indoctrinated to choose certainty, to choose anything other than being open to the possibility of not knowing and simply exploring our passions and potential to see where our path might lead us.

Jim Carrey summed it up perfectly on why we should pursue our purpose in his speech to the students graduating from Maharishi University of Management in 2014.

"So many of us choose our path out of fear disguised as practicality. What we really want seems impossibly out of reach

For many of us, our true creative potential was never unleashed. It was repressed instead of expressed and at best, tolerated.

and too ridiculous to expect, so we never dare to ask the universe for it. I'm proof that you can ask the universe for it. My father could have been a great comedian, but he didn't believe that it was possible for him. So, he made a conservative choice instead. He got a safe job as an accountant, and when I was 12 years old he was let go from that safe job and our family had to do whatever we could to survive. I learnt many great lessons from my father, not the least of which was that you can fail at what you don't want, so you might as well take a chance at doing what you love."

Purpose is all about taking a chance at doing what really matters to you. It's about doing what you love, despite what everyone around you may be telling you.

As a mother, I want nothing more than to see my son create a vocation out of his passions. That's why I believe it's vital to ask youth a different question than the standard question of what they want to be when they grow up. We should be asking them what they love to do, make or create and then help them curate a livelihood around that.

As adults, while we're asking our kids this question, surely we must be asking it of ourselves too?

So, if historically, the industrial age and our education system diverted us away from meaning and purpose, what does the future look like?

THE FUTURE OF PURPOSE

I believe that if you don't derive a deep sense of purpose from what you do, if you don't come radiantly alive several times a day, if you don't feel deeply grateful at the tremendous good fortune that has been bestowed on you, then you are wasting your life. And life is too short to waste.

- Srikumar Rao

The Human Age is happening right now for a few very powerful reasons. Firstly, we're waking up from the slumber of the consumer/worker mentality inculcated through the industrial age. We're becoming more conscious of our desire to be fulfilled as wholehearted human beings where the boundaries between work, life and play are blurred.

And as I wrote in the introduction of this book, recent world events have brought us to the apex of this age. Like never before we're each being called to step up and become activists in our daily lives and, therefore, activists for humankind.

OUR NEEDS HAVE EVOLVED

In *Liberating the Corporate Soul*, Richard Barrett builds on Maslow's Hierarchy of Needs and suggests that all actions attempt to satisfy one of four needs: physical, emotional, mental or spiritual and that these needs correspond with one of nine basic human motivations.

Human Needs	Personal Motivation
Spiritual	9. Service
	8. Making a Difference
	7. Meaning
Mental	6. Personal Growth
	5. Achievement
Emotional	4. Self-esteem
	3. Relationships
Physical	2. Health
	1. Safety

At the physical level, we're motivated by having our basic health and safety needs met and we tend to be self-focused. As we move through the stages of motivation we become other-focused where we desire meaning and to be of service. This is where many of us are evolving into right now and it's why we're seriously questioning the value of the work we're doing and the impact it's having.

THE WORLD OF WORK HAS EVOLVED

At another level, the world of work as we once knew it has radically changed. We can no longer count on the idea of a stable, life-long career in one industry or with one company. Statistics suggest that the average person will change their career around 5-7 times during their working life. With an ever-increasing number of different career options, about a third of the total workforce will change jobs every 12 months. Astonishingly, by the age of 42 most people will have already had about 10 jobs.

Today, technology is enabling us to work from anywhere, create anything we wish to and earn a living outside of traditional employment. We're choosing to create 'portfolio livelihoods' where our income is derived from multiple sources. We're being enabled to make money from a range of passions while also doing work that's not necessarily meaningful in order to pay the bills.

And then there's the automation of the workforce. If 47% of jobs are going to be automated by 2034, what does that mean for our work future? We'll each be called to develop new talents and skills to serve the changing needs of the world and our own needs while we're at it!

TECHNOLOGY ENABLES HIGHER PURPOSE

Companies with a long history are spending billions of dollars on technology in order to remain relevant and competitive, while emerging companies are being built on technological foundations.

Both, however, may simply be using technology to exacerbate the deep flaws in capitalism, in two ways. Firstly, by building products that create unnecessary western-world wants and that inflict harm on humanity and the environment instead of using technology to solve real world problems. Secondly, by using technology to extract wealth from the majority to benefit the few, instead of sharing wealth equitably so that everyone prospers.

The moral and ethical conundrum leaders face right now is how to divert their technological endeavours towards balancing the imperative of profit with a higher purpose and thereby ultimately contributing to the reparation of capitalism.

Technology is also bringing transparency to many unethical and immoral institutional and governmental practices and systems through global activist organisations like Wikileaks and AVAAZ and through alternative media sources and citizen journalism. As our values and beliefs are being assaulted, we're waking up and we're no longer willing to be passive about it. The citizens are mobilising and they're using technology to build co-operatives, businesses and community groups that side-step dominant capitalist and financial systems.

The future of work, thanks to technology, is here now and we have no choice but to evolve. Combine a higher purpose with technology and we have the potential to radically heal humanity and the planet.

If 47% of jobs are going to be automated by 2034, what does that mean for our work future? We'll each be called to develop new talents and skills to serve the changing needs of the world and our own needs while we're at it!

In fact, I predict that in the next five years, the biggest disruption in the world will not come from advancements in technology, but from advancements towards purpose, where technology will merely be the great enabler of purpose.

In fact, I predict that in the next five years, the biggest disruption in the world will not come from advancements in technology, but from advancements towards purpose, where technology will merely be the great enabler of purpose.

PURPOSE DRIVES PROSPERITY

Imbue your money with soul, your soul, and let it stand for who you are, your love, your work and your humanity.
- Lynne Twist

OUR MONEY MIND-SET

Clearly money is a highly valuable commodity. We need it to live on, to pay the bills and to look after our families (at least while it's the primary form of currency). It's also a form of energy that generates either negativity or positivity in our lives. This has absolutely nothing to do with how much we have and everything to do with our attitude and behaviour with money.

If we acquire it and use it mindfully, we feel good about our choice. If we acquire it unethically or use it recklessly, at worst, it can destroy us. Money always brings with it, its own karma – whether that's at an individual level or an organisational level.

There are also two major erroneous beliefs that many people have around money. The first one is that our net-worth is equal to our self-worth. How much we have and what we own becomes the measure of how we value ourselves and how we believe others value us.

The second belief is that 'he who has the most, wins'. This comes from a lack mind-set, a belief that there is simply not enough to go around and that in order for me to have more, you must have less. It's like being trapped in a game of Monopoly where the winner takes all and every other player loses.

Money can either enslave us or free us. A purpose-driven work life is one that empowers us to build things from a true sense of freedom which includes releasing ourselves from the normative beliefs we've been fed around money and its purpose. When we need less, we are free to create more, give more and serve more. This does not mean that we do not value money or live like a pauper. It means that we value what it enables, no matter the amount.

CULTIVATING A PROSPERITY MIND-SET

Some have referred to this next great age as 'the purpose economy'. I'm personally averse to the idea of attaching the word 'economy' to purpose. (Economy refers to the state of a country or region in terms of the production and consumption of goods and services and the supply of money.) For me, connecting purpose to economy limits the power and potential of a higher purpose. I prefer the idea of generating 'prosperity' through purpose which is a more holistic notion.

I believe that prosperity is actually the twin sister of purpose – the other side of the same coin.

Prosperity is defined as a state of flourishing, thriving and good fortune. Prosperity encompasses wealth but also includes other factors independent of wealth, such as happiness and health. In fact, in Buddhism, prosperity is viewed with an emphasis on collectivism and spirituality. Prosperity implies that everyone benefits including, most critically, our Mother Earth.

I love the Buddhist emphasis on collectivism as the foundation of prosperity. Prosperity is where purpose and profit merge into one and where everyone is doing well and everyone has enough.

At an organisational level, prosperity implies that all stakeholders collectively benefit from the value created by the organisation, which includes employees, customers, shareholders, suppliers, partners, the community and the environment.

> When we need less, we are free to create more, give more and serve more. This does not mean that we do not value money or live like a pauper. It means that we value what it enables, no matter the amount.

Prosperity implies that there is 'equity' in the distribution of wealth, not necessarily 'equal' distribution. Equity is about fairness and ensuring that everyone involved in the bringing of goods and services to market is not just surviving but thriving.

I don't delve into the topic of money and prosperity in this course although it's the most important work for you to do alongside the purpose work. I recommend reading *The Soul of Money* by Lynne Twist, as her philosophies are very much aligned with those in this book.

Living a life of freedom and purpose does not require great wealth. It requires a re-evaluation of what's really most important to you and how you can work towards collective prosperity while free in the knowledge that there's enough for everyone.

Journal for 30 minutes answering these questions.

What do you feel about the words profit, money, income, wealth, prosperity? How are they different? What are some of the limiting beliefs you need to shake?

How did you acquire, spend, save your money last year? List specifics. How do you feel about that?

Describe your overall energy and feelings around money? Are you satisfied with it? If not, how would you like to feel about money?

How much money is actually enough for you?

ROBERT'S STORY

 The world is but a canvas to our imagination.
- Henry David Thoreau

Robert Davis is a dear friend of mine who I met five years ago in Melbourne. He's a tall, handsome American and a most exquisite fine artist. Robert has lived and worked all over the world from Philadelphia to Shanghai to Melbourne and now in London.

When I first met Robert, he'd just moved to Melbourne and was barely making ends meet. On occasions, he was working for cash as a day-hire labourer knocking down walls on construction sites and living extremely frugally on just $10 a day.

While he'd enjoyed a good deal of success with his art and made a healthy income in Shanghai teaching and exhibiting his own work, he'd come to Melbourne with little means and he was starting all over again. As Robert says, "It was sobering and humbling and really soul destroying. I wasn't in a very good place for that first couple of years. I had a suitcase full of capabilities and many past successes under my belt but there weren't many doors opening".

Robert clearly recalls the first day we met. "You asked me, 'why do you do what you do? What is your purpose? What difference are you making with your art?' I'd never been asked such direct questions before and it shook me up a bit. It started me thinking about the real value and impact of my work," says Robert.

After this experience, Robert decided to take bigger and bigger steps into building a business around his art and to seek fair compensation for his services.

"It was a real turning point for me," says Robert, "I regained my confidence and belief in myself and my work and around the same time I also met my life partner and Melbourne became the place to always come home to (Robert is now an Australian citizen). Things just seemed to fall into place."

Since then, Robert has shared his story on two TEDx stages, completed numerous well-paid fine-art life-landscapes of people's life stories and taken up a role as the art teacher at the prestigious American School in London until mid 2017.

While teaching art and painting landscapes for clients, he's also never once stopped creating his own art. One of his recent pieces was chosen for the poster of The Art Below Summer Show which was seen by millions of people in the London Underground. This has led to the creation of a bespoke piece of art for the founder of Art Below (he was chosen out of hundreds of artists), his own exhibition in London and the landing of an art rep who will present his work all over the UK.

In terms of his work as an art teacher, he's also made a real impact on his students. He now asks them what they want to do with their art out of school and more importantly 'why' and he shows them how to make art an integral part of their lives. Every student is asked to write, 'I am full of possibilities…' in their art journal on their very first lesson.

And in parent/teacher interviews he even asks parents about their *why*. "I say to them… 'I know what makes your kid happy, but what makes you happy? Are you doing work that you are truly passionate about?'" says Robert. "I even had one father tear up when I asked that question. He shared that he was extremely unhappy in his career and that his whole life he'd loved drawing and that he'd always wanted to be an architect."

What I love most about Robert's story is that he has never, ever given up on his purpose and the fact that he's been flexible and adaptable in bringing it to life. He has three projects that each make him a healthy livelihood: employment as an art teacher, his business in bespoke commissioned work and then his public exhibitions and sales.

 Watch Robert Davis' talk on The Slow School of Business YouTube channel.

THE PURPOSE PROJECT

> *It takes half your life before you discover that life is a do-it-yourself project.*
> - Napoleon Hill

Robert's story is a great segue into the reason this course is called *The Purpose Project*. Robert treats his life and the way he earns a living as a series of projects. Each piece of art is a project. Each exhibition is a project. Even his time as a teacher at The American School in London has been a project as he ends his contract to start new projects back in Australia. Each project is a stepping stone to another project that fulfils his purpose.

If you've never really thought about your *why* before, or taken any action towards exploring it, it can be hard to conceive how you might find it and bring it to life. That's why we start by adopting bite-sized projects to test our potential path.

We think of our work as a series of projects, each with a start and end date and a way to measure our sense of joy, satisfaction and success. Even within the scope of a long career at one organisation, *Purpose Projects* are a great way to affect change in your daily work and make an impact on those around you.

Projects enable us to test, proto-type and experiment with our purpose. A project might simply involve self-directed learning and researching a field you're passionate about and then completing an assignment to assess if you've found that thing that lights you up.

For example, if your desire has always been to be a veterinarian, before enrolling in a four-year course, it simply makes sense to take on your own project to test its viability. This could involve creating a vision for what that career might look like and a deep dive into *why* you want to be a vet. It might involve working at your local vet voluntarily or with the RSCPA while learning all you can about the profession through online resources and documentaries. It could involve spending time with vets and interviewing them about the reality of the life of a vet. There's nothing like learning through an experiential project before committing to the rigorous education required for some professions.

THE WHAT & THE WHY

When you undertake any project, you first need to understand *what* it is you want to achieve and more importantly, *why* you want to achieve it. When you are convicted of your *why*, the *what* always transpires, most often not *how* you'd envision it or at the exact time you might have hoped for, but usually it eventuates.

This book is a great example of that and it's a testament to the fact that I'm 'on purpose'. The moment I conceived the idea in late 2015, I knew that it would come to fruition, that I had the experience and know-how to write it and that, most importantly, it met my purpose to write books that truly matter.

My *Purpose Project* became to write *The Purpose Project* (although it had a different title at the time). In January 2016, I set about writing the first 5,000 or so words. As I was writing, I gained more clarity on who it was for and the content. I wasn't even thinking about how I would publish it or market it.

Then in late July 2016, after a number of life and work distractions, I realised that I'd not really progressed the book as much as I'd hoped. So, I organised a week-long lock-up in a cottage in the bush with the goal to finish 20,000 words and a marketing proposal to send to three potential publishers.

Even at the time of sending out the proposals on the final eve of that lock-up, I was unattached to how the book would eventually be published or who would publish it. It was just one more stepping stone to fulfilling my vision.

Not long after sending out the proposals, I received an email from one of the publishers rejecting my proposal. "Purpose is peaking and there are a number of books being launched in 2017 on purpose, so you've missed the boat," I was told.

This rejection was all the impetus I needed to finish this book and self-publish it. I wasn't deterred one little bit. In fact, I was even more motivated by this rejection which I saw as just another sign that I'm doing work that really matters.

The point of this story is that when we know *what* we want to achieve and *why*, we can be less dogmatic about the *how*.

Incidentally, when I ask the question to a room full of people, "how many of you would like to write and publish a book?", I guarantee at least a 50% show of hands. When I ask, "how many have written a book?" about 5% will respond with a "yes". When I ask, "who has actually published it (self-published or commercially)?" the numbers go down to about 1%.

So often, what we say we really want, is not actually what we want. If we wanted it that badly, we'd already have done it or at least be doing it.

When we know our *why,* we simply have work to do, even when there is absolutely no guarantee of success.

Purpose Projects don't only work at an individual level. They work well for teams and across organisations and stakeholder groups too. Collective projects based on activating a higher purpose are the way to transform cultures and bring life back to the workplace.

The ultimate goal of this book is to help you pick a *Purpose Project* or projects to accomplish something that is both meaningful to you and that serves your corner of the world. The aim is to help you gain clarity of purpose through the completion of a project by giving you the tools and structures you need.

> When we know our *why,* we simply have work to do, even when there is absolutely no guarantee of success.

SETTING YOUR INTENTION

 Our intention creates our reality.
- Wayne Dyer

There's a reason you bought this book. Perhaps it's because the work path you're currently pursuing is not fulfilling you? Or perhaps you know that you have a latent creative talent burning away inside that must be unleashed? Or maybe you're in transition in your life?

Whatever your reason for buying this book, if you're going to read it, you might as well commit to doing something with it. This is the part where you define what you want from undertaking this course.

You may be wondering why the intention setting was not at the beginning of this book? The reason is that if you've got this far, I'm assuming something is really resonating for you and that, therefore, you'll be passionate about doing this work. You'll at least have some idea of what you're in for and understand what you're committing to.

This book is not here to help you tie up your work future in a neat little box in no time. It's designed to set you on a path to follow to discover the work that's right for you. In doing this work, there's no end goal to achieve, no destination, no full stop, just a series of practices to adopt and a series of projects to take on. We become daily practitioners of purpose.

GIVE YOURSELF PERMISSION

Life begins at the end of your comfort zone.
- Neale Donald Walsch

This work is messy and uncomfortable. You'll need to get comfortable with being uncomfortable. You'll have to step out of those old patterns that keep you stuck and do things you've never done before. You'll need to reconnect with those things that you truly loved before life took over.

You'll have to take a stand for yourself to do this work and not let other people's priorities usurp your commitment. You'll have to become a citizen of your own world and not wait for permission to be granted by the powers that be – whether that's your partner, children, parents, teachers or your boss.

As long as you're not hurting anyone, the only permission you need is your own.

Remember those old 'permission slips' you used to have to get from your parents when absent from school? You need to write yourself one of those and give yourself permission to take a day off work, to stop working 60 hours a week to make time for it, to make Sunday your day for this work, to do something radical to break your conditioned patterns, to spend regular breaks in nature, to meditate and write in your journal.

The permission slip is a way to release yourself from all the excuses you might have for not doing this work. It means you won't be punished for being absent from school/work/family and any other thing that might stop you. Every time you feel torn about spending time on it, get out your permission slip and re-read it.

It might seem a little silly, but let's do it. Write yourself a permission slip. In fact, write yourself a whole page of permission slips. Write about all the things you're giving yourself permission for while doing this work.

Dear Me,

I give you permission to...
I give you permission to...
I give you permission to...
I give you permission to...
I give you permission to...

Love Me

WRITING YOUR STATEMENT OF INTENTION

Now that you've given yourself permission, it's time to set an intention for what you want to achieve from this course.

Your *Statement of Intention* is your vow to undertake this work. It's about why you're doing this course, the qualities you'll bring to this work, how you'll look after yourself so this work can flourish and it's about agreeing on some dates and times that will fit in with your schedule.

I encourage you to be kind to yourself in setting your intentions and timelines. We're all at different ages and life stages with varying commitments, so I'd much rather you go slowly and take a year or more to do this course than go fast, burn out and give up. Confucius says, "it does not matter how slowly you go, as long as you don't stop."

Set your intentions mindfully after deep reflection over a period of days. The more robust the promises you make to yourself, the more likely you are to fulfil them. You may or may not wish to share your intentions with others, but if it is helpful, then do it. Please also be mindful not to compare where you are at, with others. Comparisons are never, ever helpful.

> We're all at different ages and life stages with varying commitments, so I'd much rather you go slowly and take a year or more to do this course than go fast, burn out and give up. Confucius says, "it does not matter how slowly you go, as long as you don't stop."

Write down the answers to the following questions.

My intention in doing this course is to...
(Why are you doing this course?)

My daily routine to do this work looks like...

I will approach this work with...
(What qualities will you bring to this work? E.g. love, grace, humour, forgiveness, non-judgement, passion, self-compassion, self-love. What do each of these qualities mean for you?)

I will practise the following self-care while doing this course...
(What self-care will you undertake during this course? E.g. daily gym, meditation, yoga, healthy eating, no alcohol. Be gentle on yourself here, just choose one or two things that you know have limited your potential in the past.)

I will complete this course by ___/___/___.

I will spend_____ hours per week on this course at the following times _____.

I will tell the following people I'm doing this work...
(Be careful who you choose. List the names of people you will tell, e.g. your parents, friends, partner. What am I asking from them to support me?)

I will get professional support in doing this work from...
(List the names of people you will work with on this course, e.g. a coach, friend, co-worker, mastermind group.)

I will have an outline of my *Purpose Project* and be starting it
by ___/___/___.

(Include any other statements, aims, goals that have not been covered by
the above.)

Signed

Name

Date _____/_____/_____

FROM INTENTION TO ACTION

So now you've written your *Statement of Intention*, take a day or two to
reflect on it before making any changes you need to. While you're free to
change your intention at any time down the track, I don't advocate it unless
it's absolutely necessary. Sticking to your intention is a way of testing how
capable you are of keeping your promises to yourself.

Now that you've written it freehand or in your online journal, get creative
and reproduce it on coloured paper, either printed or handwritten. Add
colours, images or whatever works for you. Then make it accessible so
you can refer to it at any time. Place it on your bathroom mirror, office
pin-up board, your work desk or in the front of your journal, or all of the
above.

Once you've set your intention, now is the time to act on it. Set up your
diary with the dates, times and activities you've committed to. Make a
time to meet with the people you need for support or your purpose buddies
or mastermind group. Create your ideal week to ensure the work gets done.

Then try things out. If they work, take note and do more of that. If they
don't work, change them but only after you've tested them properly. This

doesn't mean that if it's uncomfortable, you should change things. If it's uncomfortable, you're probably meant to be doing those things. A state of perturbation and disruption is essential for change and growth to occur.

And hey, finally, don't take it all so seriously. Have fun with it. While the purpose work is definitely not easy work, it's meant to be done with love and compassion for yourself and a sense of lightness.

Now it's time to get down to it and start your purpose journey. Thanks so much for finding the courage to join me and the other courageous cause leaders featured in this book. We're here with you all the way!

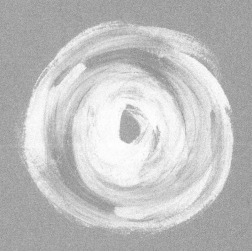

PART 2

DISCOVERING YOUR PERSONAL WORK PURPOSE

FINDING YOUR WORK PURPOSE

" Efforts and courage are not enough without purpose and direction. "
- JF Kennedy

You may feel that finding your purpose-driven livelihood is a utopian dream. Perhaps you feel that nothing you've done to date could possibly lead you to your purpose or that you just don't have what it takes to do the work you'd really love to be doing.

Our work purpose is not found in a new job, a new company or a new country. It's actually much closer than we think and it's right there already, we just haven't been paying attention and tending to it.

The story of the Golden Buddha puts this idea into perspective.

UNEARTHING YOUR GOLDEN BUDDHA

In 1957, an entire Monastery in Thailand was being relocated by a group of monks. One day as they were shifting a giant clay Buddha from its foundations, one of the monks noticed a large crack in the clay. On closer inspection, he observed a golden light emanating from the crack. The monk used a hammer and a chisel to chip away at the layers of clay until he revealed that the entire statue was made of solid gold.

Historians believe the Buddha had been covered with clay by Thai monks several hundred years earlier to protect it from being stolen in an attack by

> Our work purpose is not found in a new job, a new company or a new country. It's actually much closer than we think and it's right there already, we just haven't been paying attention and tending to it.

Through an awareness of, and deep acceptance of our past, we start to shape something meaningful for our future. We start to unearth and reclaim our own Golden Buddha.

Burmese warlords. In the attack, all the monks had been killed and it wasn't until 1957 that this great treasure was discovered.

This true story is a metaphor for our life.

I believe we are each born a Golden Buddha, but during the course of our life we get covered in layer upon layer of clay. The clay is a metaphor for our unconscious conditioning to conform and our life circumstances. The first layer of clay appears the moment we're born with gender conditioning. Then further layers of clay are added by parents, culture, religion, society, the media, schools and workplaces.

But the heaviest layer of clay is of our own doing. It's our acceptance of this unconscious conditioning which results in our limited thinking and unfulfilled potential. We become so laden with clay that we forget our Golden Buddha is there all the time.

Then one day a crack appears in the clay due to painful life circumstances such as ill health, the death of a loved one, job loss or divorce. In this moment, we wake up, we become conscious. We become deeply aware of the crack and we get a wee glimpse of our own unique golden light.

From here we start to chip away at the clay by asking ourselves the most profound questions that we've avoided for far too long. We start to rediscover those things we were passionate about as we grew up. We reconnect with why we first went into our profession or that job we really loved. We recall the times when we were 'in flow' and time stood still. We explore more deeply those latent creative talents we were born with. We reflect on those times that were both joyful and painful. We start to feel, and then truly believe, that something new and brilliant is lying below waiting to emerge.

Through an awareness of, and deep acceptance of our past, we start to shape something meaningful for our future. We start to unearth and reclaim our own Golden Buddha.

Imagine a world where every person could return to their natural state, their Golden Buddha. Wouldn't that be something?

Journal for 30 minutes about your Golden Buddha and the layers of clay that you've unconsciously accepted over the years.

What are the layers of clay that need removing and why?

Why is it important for you to start exploring your *why*?

What would each day feel like for you exploring your purpose?

DISCOVER YOUR IKIGAI

The only way to do great work is to love what you do.
- Steve Jobs

As mentioned, the Japanese term for purpose is 'ikigai'. It means 'reason for being'. They believe that everyone has an ikigai and that finding it requires a deep and lengthy search of self to find it. The term is composed of two Japanese words, *iki* referring to life, and *gai* which means 'the realisation of what one expects and hopes for'.

They believe that exploring your ikigai is integral to leading a fulfilling and wholehearted life. Ikigai gives people a reason to enjoy life and a reason to get up in the morning. This reason is not linked to external circumstances. Even if the present is dark and tragic, as long as you have a reason for being, you will survive. There's a very strong correlation between the work of Frankl's *Man's Search for Meaning* and ikigai.

So how do we discover our ikigai? We start with the ikigai purpose model on the following page.

Purpose is found at the intersection of **what you are good at** (strengths, skills, talents), **what you love** (passions, loves, where you lose track of all time), **what the world needs** (making a difference, serving others, healing humanity, regenerating the planet/environment) and **what you can be paid for** (a job or task performed for money).

This model becomes the basis for unearthing your personal work purpose. Through deep enquiry and exploration of each of these circles working with mindful, well-considered questions, you can start to uncover what's most important to you and those things that might lead to your calling. The ikigai model forms the central theme of the work in this book and the journaling questions coming up.

Discover Your Purpose

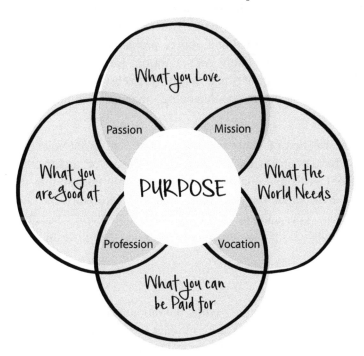

The Japanese Ikigai model for finding purpose.

WHAT YOU CAN BE PAID FOR

If you're working solely in this circle, you're likely to be just turning up for the money to pay the bills. You're unlikely to be using your skills and talents doing what you love or what the world needs. It's okay to be working just in this circle. There's no judgment here. We've all done this and many do it so we can pursue our unpaid passions outside of our paid work.

Many 'purpose-driven' people find themselves working in all the other circles but this one. While they're truly lucky to have found their guiding north-star, the goal for these people is to work intensively on this circle to develop ingenious and creative ways to make a healthy income from their work.

WHAT YOU ARE GOOD AT

This is where your strengths, skills and talents are being fully utilised and you're being sought out for them. You're experienced, knowledgeable, qualified and well-regarded and you've probably spent years cultivating these talents. You most likely get sought out for the things you're good at: selling, marketing, writing, teaching, website building, carpentry, plumbing, graphic design, bookkeeping, financial planning, nursing and so on.

At the intersection of 'what you are good at' and 'what you can be paid for', you have a 'profession'. A profession is a paid occupation that makes use of your skills and qualifications. People only operating in these two circles can be quite rational, functional and career-driven. Over time, burn-out can occur and you start to question it all, mainly because you've been unable to incorporate the other two circles of purpose into your work.

WHAT YOU LOVE

In this circle, you're moving beyond the rational and functional, where the first two circles keep you. You're moving into serious heart territory. It's where you start to lose track of time and are inspired by your work. You're in flow because the work you're doing fuels your fire. It's where you feel like you're accomplishing something that's really meaningful to you.

'What you are good at' and 'what you love' are not the same thing. For example, if you're a talented engineer you can use your skills to design yet another high-rise office block that you've done many times before, or you can use your skills to design a revolutionary new water theme park that tests your talents and that gives you real joy.

At the intersection of 'what you are good at' and 'what you love', you find your 'passion'.

WHAT THE WORLD NEEDS

When you add this circle to the other three circles, then absolutely anything is possible. This is when your work is also of service to others. It's no longer about 'me'. It's about 'we'. You're using your skills and talents to accomplish something that is meaningful to you and that is consequential for the world.

For example, imagine if the engineer were to use his skills to design a water theme park that could not only bring joy to families that could afford it, but to families living in poverty? Or imagine if the theme park had a water and environmental education aspect to it or a program to bring water wells to developing countries facing water crises?

At the intersection of 'what you love' and 'what the world needs', you've found your 'mission'. A mission is an assignment you simply have to achieve that is not necessarily financially rewarded. Many charity volunteers are actually on a mission.

At the intersection of 'what the world needs' and 'what you can be paid for', you've found your 'vocation'. A vocation is a worthy occupation that pays you while you solve world problems but does not necessarily make the most of 'what you are good at' or 'what you love'.

WHAT CIRCLES ARE YOU WORKING IN?

When it comes to our work, most of us only play in one or two of these circles at a time and mostly in the circles of 'what you can be paid for' and 'what you are good at'. Many people have never considered how they might incorporate the 'what you love' and 'what the world needs' circles into their work.

You may feel it's impossible to fulfil all four circles in one job. That's not the immediate aim. The goal is to gently explore all these circles and bring them to the fore so they can all dance together over time. The aim is to be curious not serious, to have fun and test things out. Over time, we aim to fulfil our potential and purpose by activating all four circles.

Before I gave everything up and moved to France in 2010, I was in a profession, doing what I was good at and could be paid for. I'd never deeply considered what I

You may feel it's impossible to fulfil all four circles in one job. That's not the immediate aim. The goal is to gently explore all these circles and bring them to the fore so they can all dance together over time.

truly loved or what the world needed or how these might be integrated into my work.

The time in France was the career-circuit breaker I needed to explore and experiment with these other two circles and it was the foundation for changing the trajectory of my life's work. However, as I've already stated, you don't need to run away from home like I did, to find your *why*. You can start right where you are, with all that you have in your current work.

Keep reading for a list of questions to journal on that will help you explore each of these circles in depth.

LAURA'S STORY

Recently I had a coffee with a 45-year-old corporate employee, Laura. She looked tired and sad and there was a general air of helplessness and hopelessness about her. We discussed her work and it was immediately clear that she was most definitely working in the circles of 'what she is good at' and 'what she can be paid for'.

She was talented, educated, highly qualified and a very productive team player. If there was something that needed to be done, she was the one that got the job. "I often work at least 50 hours a week," she told me, "the company pays me really well but my boss really doesn't value me. We're all so focused on bringing in the next contract that no one really thinks about the impact we're having as a company. Making money is our only priority," she shared.

We discussed her personal life and how she spent her time out of work which was mostly spent caring for her elderly parents, being a supportive wife and a devoted mother (and taxi-service) to her teenage kids. She also mentioned numerous friends dealing with problems that she'd made herself available to.

Laura had been doing everything for everyone else for many years and had devoted literally no time to exploring the things that would bring her real joy.

This is a classic case of the 'what you love' and 'what the world needs' circles being totally usurped by the others. Laura has been over-serving others and under-serving herself, which is my definition of martyrdom. While one might argue that she's doing what the world needs in being of service to those who rely on her, I believe the opposite is true. It's not possible to truly serve others unless you serve yourself first.

Now Laura finds herself extremely unhappy at work, resentful of her boss and family but mostly angry at herself. "I went to a therapist the other week and she told me that I must find the courage to establish boundaries on what I will and won't do for others and to spend time on nurturing my own passions. If I don't do this, I'll burn out and then I won't be helpful to anyone, including myself," she said.

For many of us, this story may sound familiar. When I ask people what they truly love and what they're passionate about, the answer is almost never work and often limited to family or perhaps a hobby and usually something quite safe that's never really pushed them into new realms of possibility. Today, many people are so exhausted from working in jobs they hate in our workaholic world that they have very little time for family and the other necessities of life, let alone the time to explore true joy and colour wildly outside the edges of their day-to-day existence.

I truly hope that Laura found the courage to say 'no' to what was limiting her potential and 'yes' to her courage, curiosity and creativity. The most heart-warming aspect of my work is being the midwife of possibility in people like Laura. People who are ready, willing and able to get started on the purpose work constantly remind me of *why* I do what I do.

Is there a little (or big) piece of Laura's story in your story?

YOUR 50 PURPOSE QUESTIONS

Don't be afraid of the answers, be afraid of not asking the questions.

- Jennifer Hudson

Last year I went to see the great poet and philosopher, David Whyte, share his poems and philosophies at the Athenaeum Theatre in Melbourne. When he stepped onto the stage, it was love at first sight. And when he opened his mouth, it was love at first word.

For four glorious hours, the captive (mostly female) audience sat mesmerised as he teleported us right out of that theatre and into the rooms and landscapes of his life where he'd penned much of his poetry.

I was hooked from start to finish!

And the theme running throughout his magnificent oratory was, "The Beautiful Question". Throughout each poem and story, David was gently urging us to ask ourselves: what is the question you are *not* asking yourself; and, what might your life look like on the other side of that question?

Nancy Klein, author of *Time to Think,* believes that, "a wellspring of good ideas lay just beneath our untrue and limiting assumptions [our clay] and that an incisive question can remove this limiting assumption to free our mind so we can think afresh". (I highly recommend this book.)

She believes that the quality of our questions will determine the quality of our thinking and, therefore, the quality of our answers which then leads to the quality of our deeds. Continuing to ask yourself the most beautiful and insightful questions might just be the single most important idea in this book!

A WORD OF WARNING BEFORE YOU START

Coming up is a list of quality questions for you to explore and journal on based on the ikigai model.

But a word of warning before you start. Answering these purpose questions is like doing an audit of your work and life. It's a great base to start to help you unearth the latent talents and passions that already exist within you and to explore those things you've always dreamed of doing.

However, please note, your answers are only your perception of your past, not necessarily the reality. You will be likely to apply assumptions or form judgements around past experiences which you hold to be true, but are not. You may put on your 'rose-coloured' glasses and believe events were better than they may have been at the time. You may also put on your 'grey-coloured' glasses and take a more negative view of past experiences than what actually transpired. Also, if you asked your partner or a friend to answer these questions about you, chances are, they'd answer them entirely differently.

When you understand this, you can hold your answers lightly without too much seriousness and even a little bemusement. Just do the work and be mindful not to judge or berate yourself for not being good enough or achieving more. This is not helpful and will only limit your capacity to create. You are enough just as you are and you don't need fixing! You just need some healthy, fresh redirection.

You start by assessing as honestly as you can, your situation as it stands right now. Then you explore your *why* and your *what* to start creating a vision for your desired livelihood.

The gap between where you are now and where you really want to be, becomes the basis of your first *Purpose Project*. You don't need to be thinking about your project for now though. If you have ideas along the way, start a new journal page headed 'Ideas for *Purpose Projects*' and jot them down.

And now, to the questions I've curated for you!

NOTE: You can continue on with this book as you journal on these questions each day or week.

Before answering the questions perhaps there are questions you already have? Write them down. Ponder them. Are they really the questions you want answered? How might they be more thought-provoking and succinct? Add them to the list below.

The following questions are designed for you to consider on an ongoing basis and to go back to regularly. Copy them in your journal or print them out and paste them in the front of your journal. Write on one or two questions a day for 20 minutes and at least one page on each question. Don't worry if it doesn't make sense or if you are repeating yourself, just keep writing. (In fact, repetition is what you are looking for and provides a clue!)

Journaling on these questions will increase your curiosity to start playing, exploring, and prototyping. You can continue on your way through this course as you journal on these questions.

From time to time, re-read your notes and highlight those words, phrases, ideas that pop out at you or seem to be repeated.

General questions for journaling:

1. What questions do you have about your future purpose/calling/vocation?

2. Are you generally content with your work and life? Consider work, partner, family, health, spirituality, hobbies, community, finances.

3. If yes, why? If not, what are you not content with specifically?

4. If you could change anything in work or life, what would it be?

5. What is the question you are not asking yourself? What's the big question you are avoiding?

6. If money were no object and you could do anything in the world, what would it be?

7. What were the most painful experiences of your life? What lessons did you learn? How have they shaped your life? (Review your life from your earliest memories as a child to today.)

8. What were the most joyful experiences of your life? What lessons did you learn? How have they shaped your life? (Review your life from your earliest memories as a child to today.)

9. What are the stories behind the pain and joy? Where were you? Who were you with? How did you feel at the time? What was the impact of this experience? How has it played out today?

10. What important lessons have you learnt in life and what insights have you gained?

11. What did you want to 'be' when you were a kid?

12. If you could have any vocation/job in the world, what would it be?

13. What would you like people to say about you in your eulogy?

14. What are your values? List as many words as you can think of (freedom, honesty, transparency, courage, love etc) and write about how these values are expressed. Review and refine to your top 5 to 10.

15. What's the one thing you've always wanted to do, but never done?

16. What are the places or countries that you deeply desire to visit? Why?

17. Who are the people you admire the most (including people you know and people you don't know personally)? Why?

18. If you could live anywhere, where would it be? What kind of life would you be living?

19. What are the things that are holding you back from working towards your passions?

20. What are the top 20 things you desire to do before you die? Write your bucket list.

What you are good at:

Tends to be Head-based/Left Brain/Rational & Functional/ Talents/ Skills/ Strengths/Qualifications/ Experience/Knowledge

21. What strengths, skills, talents did you have as a child, teenager, adult? List as many as you've acquired over the years as possible. A skill is something you do well but may not necessarily love. It's a doing word i.e. cooking, writing, accounting, selling, designing.

22. What skills and talents have you specifically cultivated in your work life that you enjoy using? List as many as possible.

23. What skills do others most compliment you for? What do people most ask you for help with?

24. What have you studied and become intensely knowledgeable about?

25. What skills and talents would you like to continue to use and why?

What you love:

Tends to be Heart-based/Right Brain/ Emotional & Spiritual/Creative/ Passions/Beliefs/ Values/What you stand for

26. If you could spend today doing anything that you love, what would it be?

27. What are you passionate about? Write down as many things as possible that you love to do. These may be hobbies, interests or tasks at work and they can overlap with what you are good at too. Or you may not be good at it, but actually love it. Again, we are using doing words i.e. golfing, dancing, meditating, yoga, flying. Next to each word, write down why you love it. What does it provide you with?

28. What makes you lose all track of time? When are you most in flow, happy and fulfilled?

29. Where do you spend most of your time and money? Check your diary!

30. What events/things/experiences have you created in your life that you're most proud of and would consider your greatest achievements?

31. What things have you started to create in your life that have been left unfinished? Why were they unfinished?

32. What are some things you've always wanted to do or that you're curious about?

33. What would you do even if you weren't being paid for it?

34. What really, truly matters most to you? People, Places, Passions, Ideas, Interests.

35. What do you stand for and believe in? ("I believe that…" statements are very useful for getting clear on the issues/topics you are passionate about. For example: "I believe we need an education system that helps students tap into their purpose and direct their own learning.")

What the world needs:

Tends to be Full-Body Based/Other-actualised/Being of Service/Making a Difference/Being better for the world, not best in the world

36. What do you want to change or fix in your family/community/society/ company/world? What makes you angry and sad? Why is that so?

37. Why do you want to fix it? Why is that important? Why is that important? Why is that important? (Keep asking this till you drill down to the universal *why*.)

38. What would the world be/look like if you were able to change this? What would your vision for the world be?

39. How would you use your specific talents and passions to contribute to this change?

What you can be paid for:

Tends to be Head-based/Transactional/Exchange of service for money/ To be combined with what you are good at, what you love, what the world needs

40. What have you/are you currently being paid for? Write down a list of all the tasks/jobs you've undertaken in your life for which you have been paid. (It does not matter how menial or insignificant they may seem.)

41. Are you satisfied with this? If not, why not? What would you like to be paid for instead?

42. What jobs/work in your history were fulfilling for you?

43. What can you do right now to bring the other three circles into your current work? How can you start right where you are?

44. What business could you create that unites all four circles? How might you explore that?

45. What work/job/contract/voluntary role could you seek? With whom, in what industry?

Reviewing your journaling:

46. What are the key words, stories, ideas, messages that have arisen from this journaling? (Highlight those that stand out for you that are most meaningful.)

47. What are you most curious about exploring further?

48. What could you test or prototype? What ideas do you have for your *Purpose Project* now (if any)?

49. What insights have you gained from this journaling?

50. What commitment will you make to purpose journaling moving forward? Time of day, location, purpose for journaling and so on.

Write yourself a love letter:

Once you've completed your journal questions, take yourself off for half a day in nature to write yourself a love letter. Write about all the things that you're grateful for that you've created to date in your life and at work. Write on three things you're really curious about and what you'll do about them. Remind yourself why you're doing this course. Review your *Statement of Intention* and recommit to continuing this work. Sign it off with love!

Well done on getting this far! I hope that you're finding the course helpful and that you're beginning to unearth the true power of your potential.

START WHERE YOU ARE

> " *Start where you are. Do what you can.*
> *Use what you have.* "
> - Arthur Ashe

It can be unsettling once you realise you're not satisfied with the status quo and that there's something more possible for your work life. It can make one mighty restless. (If you're not restless, maybe it's a sign that you're actually pretty happy, which is cool, right?)

Remember Laura's story? It would be tempting for her to ditch her job to explore her *why;* however, it's not what I'd recommend.

Many people believe the only way to fulfil their real potential is to find another job or to start their own business. It's a natural tendency to want to run away from our pain instead of shining the spotlight on it. It's what we do in this modern world. We flee instead of sitting in the discomfort and pain of the experience and using it as an opportunity to evolve and grow. We also blame everyone else for our situation. It's not my fault that I'm doing work that makes me unhappy; it's my family's fault, my manager's fault, my leader's fault, but it's not mine.

We don't become self-leaders in finding our joy at work. We wait for others to make us happy, and if they don't, we go looking for the nearest and quickest escape route. Leadership has nothing to do with title and position and everything to do with behaviour. True leaders step up and take responsibility for changing their situation regardless of the title they hold.

> Many people believe the only way to fulfil their real potential is to find another job or to start their own business. It's a natural tendency to want to run away from our pain instead of shining the spotlight on it.

While you may be tempted to change jobs if you're unhappy, there's no guarantee whatsoever that the next job or company is going to be any better than the current one (unless you've done some serious work on your *Purpose Project*, that is.)

We're also constantly being blinded by the bright lights of entrepreneurship. If it's all too much, you can just start your own business and be your own boss, right? Freedom at last! It's estimated that 9 out of 10 start-ups actually fail. Starting your own business is 'risky business' and it requires a big investment in time and money to get it off the ground. Small business is simply not for everyone.

So, my first recommendation is to try 'coming out' instead of 'getting out'. By this I mean bringing out the 'what you love' and 'what the world needs' circles right into your current workplace. This means bringing your whole self to work not just the bits required to get the job done and meet the job description. It means bringing your own purpose to work (*BYO Purpose*) and not waiting for permission to show off the full spectrum of your passions and talents.

At this point, you may be annoyed with me and think that's just not possible, that it's a utopian dream. Perhaps you feel like chucking this book in. I hope not. I just want you to be mindful and I don't want you to quit your job tomorrow and go blindly into the horizon without having seized the opportunity that may be right in front of you, so please keep reading.

On another note, early on in this book, I shared that the future of work will be in us all having 'portfolio livelihoods' where our income will be derived from multiple sources at once. We should adopt an 'and/and' approach to our livelihood instead of an 'either/or' approach. Why not stay at work *and* start a business *and* pursue a personal passion outside of work?

And if you're already an established business owner exploring a new purpose for a new business venture, the same goes for you. There's no need to get out of your current business entirely, in order to start over, unless you have the means, confidence and clarity to go for it.

All I want you to know, is that you don't have to quit, sell everything, run away and turn your life upside down to find meaning at work. Remember, you can start right where you are, with all that you have right now.

KAREN'S STORY

 If there is a good will, there is a great way.
- William Shakespeare

About two years ago I gave a talk on purpose to the staff of a large finance company. After the talk, Karen, a financial adviser in the audience, emailed me. She told me that her real passion was health and wellbeing and that she'd been studying nutrition for the last two years. She shared that she had two years left of her study and that her co-workers and manager didn't even know that she was passionate about nutrition.

Sadly, Karen will most likely become one of those thousands of corporate escapees I was talking about in the beginning of this book. She'll leave that huge finance company and either go to work for a health company or start her own small business. Yet this needn't be the case.

What if her company were to look beyond the KPIs (Key Performance Indicators), the job descriptions and the sales targets and empower Karen to bring her own purpose to work? What if the company funded her studies and gave her time off to study? What if she was able to combine health advice with wealth advice for clients? (This would make absolute sense, as we all know that poor health can be financially devastating.) What if she could write articles on health and wellbeing for the company customer emails or run online health seminars or lunch-time group discussions for staff? What if she became the staff health & nutrition adviser?

There are literally hundreds of ways in which Karen could bring her own purpose to work. And whose responsibility is it to enable Karen do this? It's Karen's, not her manager's or any other leader's. It's up to her to step into self-leadership and bring her own purpose to life in that company. All it requires is ingenuity, creativity and a healthy dose of self-belief and gumption. By doing her research and preparing a powerful pitch (aka a *Purpose Project*) for her manager, she may just get what she really wants without having to leave the company with all the risks that might entail.

And even if her manager doesn't go for it, she'll find other leaders in the company who will see her true potential – if she has the will and dares to go find them.

From a company perspective, it makes absolute sense to enable Karen to fulfil her highest potential. Karen will become a role model to her peers and a great advocate

> *BYO Purpose* remains the greatest opportunity for companies to become an 'employer of choice' and to retain and attract the best and brightest people.

for the company, all while improving the health of her co-workers and clients. The cost of losing and having to replace talented people like Karen is enormous. *BYO Purpose* remains the greatest opportunity for companies to become an 'employer of choice' and to retain and attract the best and brightest people.

(NB: Thank you to Matt Perfect for allowing me to borrow the term *BYO Purpose*.)

Re-read your journal answers to The 50 Purpose Questions.

Pick out a couple of areas/interests that you're curious about exploring further.

Brainstorm ideas on how you might integrate them into *BYO Purpose* in your current job or company.

What might you do to test your idea/s out?

THE SIGNS OF PURPOSE

 The only real valuable thing is intuition.
- Albert Einstein

I can always tell when I'm with a person who is 'on purpose' and doing work that lights them up. They have an energy about them that draws me in. They talk with certainty and conviction. They know where they're going and they're steadfastly focused.

But how do you know if you're heading in the right direction? How do you know if you've found your raison d'être or are shifting towards it? This is where consciousness must be cultivated. We must listen to the stirrings of our own heart and feel, not think, our way through it.

Instinct and intuition are what you need to trust, not the voices in your head, or worse still, the voices of others. You have to pay vigilant attention and notice the signs that you're on the right path.

Here are just some signs that you're 'on purpose' or working towards it:

- ▶ You get tingles when you think about it. It makes you emotional.
- ▶ You don't feel like you should be doing anything else.
- ▶ You get up every morning itching to get to work.
- ▶ You incessantly think about it.
- ▶ You actually complete your 'to do' lists.
- ▶ You would do it even if you weren't getting paid.
- ▶ You have an energy, vitality and enthusiasm you never had before.

▶ Others remark on this and you inspire others to get stuck into their purpose.

▶ Synchronicity is often at play. You attract people, events or opportunities into your life in a way you never could before.

▶ People offer to help you without being asked.

▶ People share with others what you're up to. They become your advocate.

▶ You can engage others easily in a purpose conversation.

▶ You acquire new contacts, clients, networks without pushing.

▶ Other people recommend you and refer you.

▶ You're confident about taking action, even if you're uncertain of the outcome.

▶ You make decisions without overthinking or worrying.

▶ You have trust and faith that it will all work out for the best.

▶ You don't fear failure. Mistakes and losses just seem like road bumps.

▶ The *what* and the *why* is always clear to you. You don't get attached to the *how* as it evolves more fluidly and is guided more by instinct and intuition.

When you find your purpose, you will know it intuitively. Watch for the everyday signs as you undertake your daily tasks and ask yourself: am I loving what I'm doing right now; is this the only thing I desire to be doing; is it meaningful to me; is it truly helpful to others?

BECOME A PURPOSE ACTIVIST

>   " *The planet does not need more 'successful people'. The planet desperately needs more peacemakers, healers, restorers, storytellers and lovers of all kind.* "
> - Dalai Lama

Purpose doesn't need hierarchy. It's not something we need to wait for the leaders to mandate or permit. It's the one thing we can each take ownership of and responsibility for, unapologetically.

What the world needs right now are more humanists and cause leaders. We need millions and millions of heart-centred, conscious people stepping up and becoming *Purpose Activists* and bringing meaning to their daily work and to their workplaces.

While some of these people are the appointed leaders in our world, mostly they're the everyday people. They're in every corner of every company. They're in communities. They're in families. They're in schools and universities. They're in small business. They're everywhere.

And they're not just dreamers, they're doers and action takers.

They are you. You are the change-maker. What are you waiting for?

Purpose doesn't need hierarchy. It's not something we need to wait for the leaders to mandate or permit. It's the one thing we can each take ownership of and responsibility for, unapologetically.

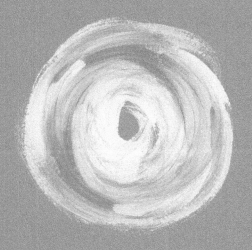

PART 3

UNEARTHING THE PURPOSE OF YOUR ORGANISATION

THE PURPOSE OF YOUR ENTERPRISE

 We need red blood cells to live (the same way a business needs profits to live), but the purpose of life is more than to make red blood cells (the same way the purpose of business is more than simply to generate profits).

- Ed Freeman

While this section is written for the business world, it's highly relevant for any collective beyond the individual: a government body, an industry association, a co-operative, a not-for-profit or charity or a social enterprise, a local community group, a school or university and even a couple or family. It's for any enterprise with a desire to be driven by a common higher purpose.

I'll use various terms for 'organisation' such as 'enterprise', 'business' or 'company' when it's appropriate. Feel free to use the word that works best for you according to the type of entity you're working with.

THE IMPERATIVE OF PURPOSE

Just like we humans, I believe most companies are born as Golden Buddhas. They're founded with a golden intent and a higher purpose; however, over time the clay appears in the form of poor management, flawed systems, hierarchical structures, board pressure or shareholder demands. The challenge for leaders is to shed the layers of clay and return the organisation to its raison d'être – its *why*.

Most leaders today are now aware of the imperative of purpose. In the HBR/EY *Business Case for Purpose* survey mentioned earlier in this book, 89% of the 474 executives interviewed, stated that they understood the importance of purpose, yet only 46% said their company actually had a strong sense of purpose. The survey concludes that purpose is a powerful though underutilised tool to transform cultures.

From a financial perspective, leaders face the issue of dealing with shareholders and investors who are often motivated solely by profit and who may not buy into the imperative of purpose. So, while they may have the financial wherewithal to go deeply into the purpose journey, there's also the challenge of having to prove its ROI (return on investment). If a higher purpose is not activated however, it will result in extensive costs associated with high employee turnover, poor productivity and performance and the loss of loyal customers who are switching to purpose-driven competitors.

Many leaders are also grappling with the best approach to take in unearthing purpose, articulating it and most importantly, making it meaningful and actionable. Additionally, they're overwhelmed at the idea that they must add 'purpose' to their already exhausting workload and responsibilities.

It can be tempting for the executive team to hand the responsibility of purpose over to HR or marketing or to an external consulting firm or ad agency. Yet there's a very real risk in 'handing over' purpose to any single team or department that only engages a select few. It will likely result in a shallow approach that does not engage people from across, up, down, inside and outside the entity, resulting in a purpose statement which becomes more of a marketing tagline rather than the company's deepest reason for existence.

That's when organisations run the risk of being seen to be 'purpose-washing' (the new 'green-washing'). Just because a company has a purpose statement does not mean they're *on* purpose. Having a purpose statement is one thing. Truly believing in it and activating it, is quite another. When the 'purpose promise' does not match the 'purpose experience' it can do more harm than good.

> If a higher purpose is not activated however, it will result in extensive costs associated with high employee turnover, poor productivity and performance and the loss of loyal customers who are switching to purpose-driven competitors.

Purpose is also an imperative to attract and keep the best

people. At any one time in a company, your people are likely to be in one of three modes: agreement, acquiescence or activism.

Purpose is also an imperative to attract and keep the best people. At any one time in a company, your people are likely to be in one of three modes: agreement, acquiescence or activism.

I believe the ones 'in agreement' are mostly the appointed leaders and those who have bought into the company strategy and vision, and most likely had a hand in creating it. These are the 13% that are 'actively engaged' in the enterprise, according to Gallup. Then the majority, around 77%, are actually 'in acquiescence' which means reluctant acceptance, not agreement. They're turning up to work each day to do what's expected of them reluctantly, but without question and they probably haven't bought into the company vision. They're likely to be the majority of those Gallup poll people who are either 'disengaged or actively disengaged' at work.

Then there's the 10% - the activists. These are the ones who question everything because they care. They want the company to have a higher purpose and be driven by something beyond profitability and productivity. They're willing to take responsibility for it - if they're empowered to do so. These people are the very ones at most risk of leaving, and the very ones the company most needs to keep. They are the *Purpose Activists*, the ones capable of starting a purpose movement that can transform cultures.

So how do you avoid 'purpose-washing'? How do you dig deep to unearth your organisational purpose to make it real and meaningful? How do you make it a truly collective purpose, one that everyone takes responsibility for?

This part of the book provides methodologies and tools for the *Purpose Activists* in a company to unearth both organisational and personal work purpose. It's a handbook for these people to start the purpose conversation in boardrooms, lunchrooms and classrooms.

That's because, profound change starts with a single courageous conversation on *why* your company exists.

DEFINING ORGANISATIONAL PURPOSE

Two years ago, I was fortunate enough to hold counsel with one of the elders of *The School of Philosophy* here in Melbourne. I was asking for advice on how I might grow *Slow School* into a purpose-driven and prosperous entity.

He shared with me his belief that the reason any organisation exists is, "to fill a need and serve the community while helping each individual find their truth and fulfil their highest potential". This profound statement irrevocably changed the way I think about any collective, whether that's a community or a business. It was also the inspiration behind my own definition of *why* any entity should exist in the first place.

The purpose of an organisation is to leave the world a better place than it was before it existed, while enabling each stakeholder in the organisation to reach their highest potential and thereby generate prosperity for all.
- Carolyn Tate

So, if this is the purpose of any collective, what then is the purpose of your community, your company or your business?

In any organisation, a higher purpose is like a higher power. It's both inside and outside the enterprise. It's both the guiding north-star, ever present yet never reachable, and the glue of the organisation, the thing that drives strategy and that drives decisions for the betterment of all stakeholders, humankind and the planet.

It answers the core questions of why we exist. How is our organisation making a positive impact and being consequential for the world? Are we serving a real human/planetary need or merely creating a superficial want? Would the world be any worse off if we didn't exist? How are we 'being better' for the world instead of striving to be 'the best' in the world? What is our ultimate reason for existence beyond profit?

The purpose of an organisation is to leave the world a better place than it was before it existed, while enabling each stakeholder in the organisation to reach their highest potential and thereby generate prosperity for all.

- Carolyn Tate

THE PROSPERITY-DRIVEN ENTERPRISE

A sustainable world means working together to create prosperity for all.
- Jacqueline Novogratz

In my experience, there's a great divide that exists between the 'for-profit' (FP) and 'not-for-profit' (NFP) or charity world. FPs have been philosophically, systemically and legally set up to prioritise profit while NFPs have been set up to prioritise purpose over profit.

Many FPs are focused on being the best and beating the competition: to have the highest stock-price, growth, market-share and profit. A company's worth is defined by their financial worth and their position on the league table.

On the other hand, the purpose of NFPs is to do good and solve world problems, most often enabled through donations from the FPs (and also government funding). While NFPs are mostly driven by a deep cause, they still experience the same challenges as their counterparts and the very same culture issues.

Many NFPs are now becoming 'social enterprises' and behaving more like FPs in order to become financially self-sufficient.

Even labelling organisations as 'for-profit', 'not-for-profit' or as a 'social enterprise' is, in my view, restrictive and creates unhelpful pre-conceptions around their ultimate reason for existence.

I believe that every organisation has the capacity to do good and make money, to become a 'profit-for-purpose' organisation and evolve into a 'prosperity-driven' entity. There is no need to sacrifice profit in the name of purpose or to sacrifice purpose in the name of profit. It's not an either/or scenario. It's about bringing these two critical ingredients for success into total equilibrium.

The Profit-for-Purpose Enterprise

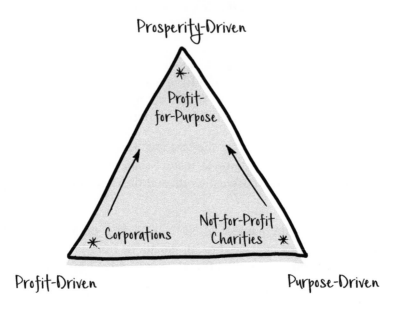

A prosperity-driven entity integrates the necessities of purpose, profit, people and the planet. It takes care of, and deeply engages, all stakeholders. It shares wealth equitably. It reinvests its profits back into the entity and its stakeholders. It shifts an organisation from a value extraction mind-set to a value regenerative mind-set. A prosperity-driven enterprise empowers everyone to take ownership, to make a contribution, to feel valued and have a sense

I believe that every organisation has the capacity to do good and make money, to become a 'profit-for-purpose' organisation and evolve into a 'prosperity-driven' entity.

of belonging. There are many successful co-operatives in the world that would classify themselves as prosperity-driven organisations.

How do we shift to being a prosperity-driven organisation? It starts with a prosperity conversation with your team by plotting where you believe your enterprise sits right now in this triangle and by discussing where you'd like to be.

(It's important to note here, that you may actually be a for-profit business but place yourself in the purpose-driven corner because you have oodles of purpose and no profit right now.)

An intriguing way to use this model is to start with the big brands. Where would you place Uber, Optus, Apple, Tesla or Facebook in this model? Why? Where could they be on this model? Get creative and list 50 ways they could become more prosperity-driven.

Then choose an organisation that is already way up on the prosperity-driven corner – perhaps study a successful global co-operative or a profit-for-purpose entity such as Patagonia, Etsy, Atlassian or even open source entities such as Wikipedia and Stocksy. You can also use it to plot and discuss your competitors against your company.

The model is a great conversation starter designed to generate creative and innovative ideas on how to shift a company to become more prosperity-driven. What comes out of these conversations can ultimately form the basis of a collective *Purpose Project*.

Get your team together and discuss this model.

Choose up to six companies (big brands, competitors, partners or suppliers) and plot them on this model. Discuss why you've placed them there.

Now plot your own company on this model. Why have you placed your company there? Plot where you think you should be.

In 30 minutes, generate at least 50 ideas that could shift your company towards prosperity. Agree on a process to filter and narrow down these ideas to your top 5 or 10.

What next steps will you take? What's a potential *Purpose Project* that could be adopted from this discussion?

PURPOSE. VISION. MISSION. VALUES.

 Wherever you go, go with all your heart.
- Confucius

Just as clarity of purpose is vital for humans to realise their full potential, so it is with any enterprise. A clear purpose drives vision, mission and values as the foundations on which to build a clear strategy.

Many organisations don't have a stated purpose and use the term 'mission' for their raison d'être instead. I believe they're very different, as are vision and values. Each of these four terms have very different meanings and serve a very different purpose. My perspective on the four terms are outlined in the humanistic model on the next page.

An organisation should think of itself as a living, breathing human being with a beating heart, a brain full of know-how and essential organs and limbs to take action.

While I've explained how this model works at an organisational level, it works equally well for your personal purpose, vision, mission and values.

> An organisation should think of itself as a living, breathing human being with a beating heart, a brain full of know-how and essential organs and limbs to take action.

Purpose . Vision . Mission . Values.

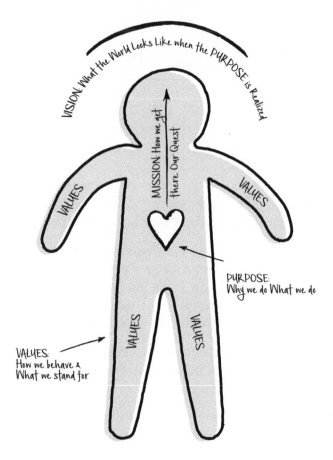

PURPOSE: WHY WE DO WHAT WE DO (THE HEART)

We start with *why*. We start in the heart. Purpose is the heartbeat of the organisation. Purpose drives vision, mission and values. It addresses *why* we exist, *why* we do what we do, how we make a difference and *why* we're here beyond making a profit.

Your purpose is both the glue and the guiding north-star. It's never fully realised and it's immeasurable. Unlike the more functional attributes of a mission, which is more head-centred, the purpose stems from emotional and spiritual attributes and is heart-centred.

Example: ThoughtWorks

To better humanity through software and help drive the creation of a socially and economically just world.

Vision: What the world looks like when the purpose is realised. (Future view)

The vision is outside the human model as it's futuristic. A vision directs the organisation beyond the day-to-day activities towards the big-picture. It answers the big *what* questions. What will the world look like when the purpose is realised? What is the vision for the company in bringing the world vision to fruition? What are we trying to achieve? There are also five senses, so consider not only what the world will look like, but what it will taste, feel, smell and sound like too.

Example: Tesla

To create the most compelling car company of the 21st century by driving the world's transition to electric vehicles.

Mission: How we get from purpose to vision. Our quest. (Heart to Head)

The mission describes what business the organisation is in and how it intends to achieve the vision. It's all about what we do and the path we take to realise our *why* to get from purpose to vision. It provides focus on how to achieve the vision through strategy and planning. It's all about the quest, ensuring we're equipped to go on the journey and being mindful of what's in our backpack on this journey. It's the *how* piece that connects the *what* and the *why*.

Unlike purpose which is heart-centred, more philosophical and intangible, the mission is more head-centred. It brings purpose to life and it's more functional, practical and actionable.

Example: Carolyn Tate & Co.

To scale the impact of The Purpose Project through mutually beneficial partnerships with major organisations that have large distribution capability.

Values: What we stand for. How we behave. (The Limbs)

Values describe the operating principles and the behaviour required in the organisation to ensure the mission is achieved. Values drive the culture. They're what keeps the body (aka the organisation) balanced, stable and moving forward. Lose a limb (in other words compromise a value) then it can seriously destabilise the mission. Many people leave organisations because the espoused values of the company are not lived. Fulfilling purpose, vision and mission is most often derailed when values are not upheld.

Example: Atlassian

Open company, no bullshit.
Build with heart and balance.
Don't #@!% the customer.
Play as a team.
Be the change you seek.

There's a great deal of art and science to unearthing and living both personal and organisational values. I recommend checking out *The Barrett Values Centre* to dig deep on company values.

Research a company that is doing great things in the world and that you aspire to be like. Dig deep on their purpose, vision, mission, values.

How are they practically bringing them to life? What evidence, stories, information do you have that support this?

What lessons have you learnt that you could adopt in your team/company?

Imagine your company is featured in the media 12 months from now after adopting a new purpose, vision, mission and values. Write a 500-word story/article and find an image and/or video to support it.

Send the article to a few of your peers to start the conversation within your team.

THE 3 LEVELS OF PURPOSE

People support what they create.
- Margaret Wheatley

Now that I've put some context around how purpose drives mission, vision and values, I'll delve even deeper into the three essential levels of purpose required to unlock human potential in your company.

When purpose is co-created, co-owned and co-activated by your people using this model, it's possible to turn a lifeless, struggling entity into an active, thriving community – a movement that has a life of its own.

3 Levels of Purpose

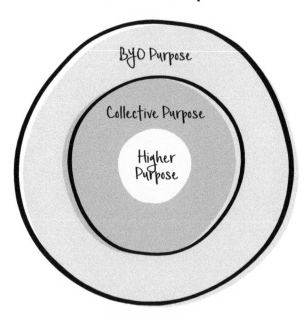

HIGHER PURPOSE

The first level is the level of higher purpose. We start by unearthing and articulating the purpose statement, ensuring it's so powerful that it becomes the rudder of the organisational ship.

> Powerful purpose statements are both inspirational and practical and should be co-created 'by the people, for the people' in partnership with leadership. For what we have a hand in creating, we take responsibility for.

Creating a new purpose statement is actually a serious *Purpose Project* in and of itself. (Keep reading for the section on how to co-create and craft a powerful purpose statement.)

Recently I spoke to a team of people at a large professional services firm. They didn't have a company purpose that they were aware of, so I asked them each privately to write down what they thought their purpose statement could be. Then I asked them to score between 1 and 10 on how motivated they were by the purpose statement they'd just written. I could see that many of them felt uncomfortable as they shared their responses. Each person had a completely different idea of the company *why* and the average motivation factor was 4.

At the end of the session, one man shared the new company-wide purpose statement that had just been released by the global executive team. The silence following the announcement was deafening and the air was thick with disinterest. Then after a period of some silence, one brave person said, "What does that even mean?" (Which was what I was actually thinking but didn't voice.)

The purpose statement was so esoteric that it was rendered meaningless. It was also evident there had been zero employee engagement in its creation. For these two reasons, this purpose will be almost impossible to activate.

Powerful purpose statements are both inspirational and practical and should be co-created 'by the people, for the people' in partnership with leadership. For what we have a hand in creating, we take responsibility for.

A co-created purpose statement then becomes a truly collective purpose, which is where the real shift happens in cultures.

THE COLLECTIVE PURPOSE

The following story is a brilliant example of a truly collective purpose.

In 1962, President Jack Kennedy was taking a tour of NASA. At one point during the tour he broke away from the tour group to greet a cleaner sweeping the floors. As they shook hands the President said "Hi, I'm Jack Kennedy, what are you doing?" to which the cleaner replied instantly, "I'm helping put a man on the moon, Mr. President".

A collective purpose is one that everybody knows and takes responsibility for and is proud of, no matter their job or title. It's one that people feel connected to and empowered to deliver on. It's one that unites all stakeholders and even inspires the competition to pick up their game. A collective purpose can be felt, seen and heard - inside and outside the entity.

So, how do you make your higher purpose a truly collective purpose?

You start a 'purpose movement' in your company by calling for the people from all corners of the company who understand the notion of higher purpose and who care deeply about it. These are the humanists, the ones already working on unearthing their own personal Golden Buddha and who are deeply immersed in their own personal growth. They're not the official leaders but the self-leaders, the *Purpose Activists* who will be intrinsically motivated to drive your *Purpose Projects*. You invite them to bring meaning to the workplace. Then you give them the tools, the nurturing and the freedom to infuse the company with meaning.

I come across potential *Purpose Activists* every single day in my work. They're the ones coming to my public courses and workshops and who are making contact with me and asking my advice. They're the soon-to-be or wannabe corporate escapees. Find them quick before they escape!

BYO PURPOSE

While you're activating the company purpose you also add another rich, deep layer to the purpose equation by enabling your people to bring their own purpose to work (*BYO Purpose*). This is where your company becomes both the arbiter and curator of individual purpose in each person, and where the ikigai purpose model is activated.

You go beyond the standard job description and the 'carrots and sticks' (rewards and punishments) and the extrinsic motivators of financial bonuses, free food, bottomless cups of coffee and groovy office fit-outs. You enable your people to dig deep to discover their intrinsic motivators.

You help them reconnect with their passion and those things that really matter to them and invite them to bring them right into their work. These may or may not be latent creative talents or interests directly related to their daily job.

(Remember the story of Karen the financial adviser? In my experience, there's literally no personal passion or interest that cannot be integrated into the workplace and our daily work.)

A few months ago, I was chatting with a young woman, Rosa, a litigation lawyer in her early 30's. She told me how much she disliked her job at her mid-sized male-dominated law firm and that she was on the verge of resigning so she could travel and start her own business.

I asked her about the times in her life where she'd really come alive and loved her work.

Her response was instant. "When I was at uni studying law, I ran a mentoring program where I brought young women studying law together with women lawyers who had graduated and were practising law. I absolutely loved it. I felt like I was making a difference and it was a real success. The women gained so much from it."

I then asked her what really bothered her about her industry and what she wanted to fix, which resulted in a deep discussion about the lack of women in leadership in law and also the destructive nature of litigation and its emotional impact on both the lawyers and their clients.

We explored ways Rosa could actually bring her passions to her current work and I challenged her to do some research and pitch a *Purpose Project* to her boss for a company sponsored 'women-in-law' mentoring program.

It makes absolute sense for us to integrate our latent talents into the workplace, and while it's up to the leaders to enable it, it's up to each individual to own it and ask for it.

To this day, I have no idea of Rosa's next steps after that conversation. I do, however, feel it's a great shame when people quit their job without first exploring how they might bring their own purpose right into their current workplace.

This is where real self-leadership comes to the fore. So many employees take a passive approach to their daily work. They do what is demanded of them, nothing more, nothing less. This makes for a dull day at work. It makes absolute sense for us to integrate our latent talents into the workplace, and while it's up to the leaders to enable it, it's up to each individual to own it and ask for it.

Rosa's example also shows that what we really love is never far from the surface. The clues are right there already. We just need to pay attention. And then we need to take action!

Give some consideration to the *3 Levels of Purpose model*.

Share the model at your next team meeting and facilitate the discussion around these questions:

Do we have a higher purpose? If so, what is it and what does it mean?

How have we made it a collective purpose? Who of our stakeholders knows it and drives it? Do we own it? What are practical examples of this?

How could we activate *BYO Purpose* at work?

THE (HIGHER) PURPOSE STATEMENT

> *To some people, power is a noun. To others, it's a verb.*
> - Andre Carson

THE PURPOSE STATEMENT FRAMEWORK

Now to that elusive higher purpose statement, the epi-centre of the three levels of purpose and where it all starts. The best statements are inspirational and heart-centred while being practical and actionable. They're not necessarily the most cleverly worded, but they're sincere and authentic. They're written straight, not great. In fact, if they're too clever, they can be misconstrued as simply the latest ad slogan instead of the raison d'être.

Meaningful purpose statements generally include three core elements following a clear framework as shown in the following model: a verb; an intention; and an outcome or beneficiary.

Not all great purpose statements follow this model exactly but the framework is a good place to start. We use the model to choose word options for the statement and then ensure each element has a meaning, some rationale and a story to support it.

Let me demonstrate this framework on my own company purpose which is 'to unearth a higher purpose in people and organisations'. We use the 'options' boxes to get creative and select various words that could be used as an alternative to 'unearth' (e.g. discover, uncover, excavate). A thesaurus is a brilliant tool to find verb options.

> Meaningful purpose statements generally include three core elements following a clear framework as shown in this model: a verb; an intention; and an outcome or beneficiary.

The Purpose Statement Framework

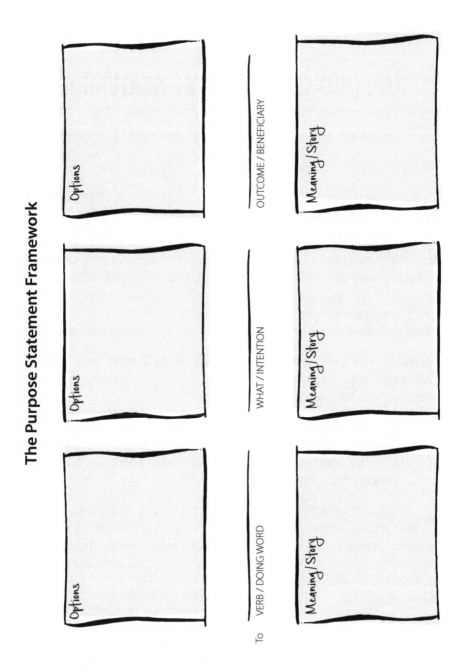

Here's a list of great verbs to get you started:

Accelerate, Activate, Advance, Awaken, Become, Better, Bring, Build, Co-create, Connect, Consolidate, Create, Cure, Design, Do, Empower, Enable, End, Engage, Further, Give, Grow, Fertilise, Ignite, Inspire, Kick-start, Make, Prevent, Project, Promote, Rebuild, Regenerate, Reimagine, Reinvent, Retain, Revolutionise, Share, Spread, Start, Stimulate, Surge, Unearth, Unleash.

I chose 'unearth' because it says that your purpose is already there to be dug up and that you don't have to go looking outside for it. I can also tell numerous stories around the verb 'unearth' like the Golden Buddha story. The what/intention part of that statement is 'a higher purpose'. I have used 'higher purpose' and not just 'purpose' so I can share what is implied by that word 'higher' (higher power, higher than profit, higher than ourselves) and also define what purpose means.

And the final part of the statement 'people and organisations' shows who I serve. It connects personal purpose to organisational purpose and enables a conversation on why both are essential. I had considered changing 'people and organisation' to 'workplace'; however, I felt it precluded 'education' – a sector that I'm particularly passionate about serving. As you can see, there is a real art and science to crafting a statement that is meaningful.

At a recent *Purpose Project* workshop that I ran, two people from the same tech company were in attendance. They went away separately to work on their statement and came back with totally different statements with totally different sentiments. It was an excellent conversation starter and it revealed just how at odds their perspectives were on the company *why*. They left the workshop with a commitment to take on their first *Purpose Project* which was to co-create a company purpose statement that everyone could own and love.

Another woman who attended the workshop, an employee of a major Australian company, used the framework to create her own personal purpose statement to bring to her daily work.

EXAMPLES OF GREAT PURPOSE STATEMENTS

Below is a list of just some of my favourite purpose statements for organisations I admire and respect. See how they work against the suggested framework I've put forward.

Note: You may wish to drop the word 'To' and just add 'ing' to the verb as an alternative. E.g. 'Awakening the best in people and organisations.'

KeepCup	To kick-start the demise of the disposable cup.
Wake Up Project	To awaken the best in people and organisations.
Interface Carpets	To become fully sustainable with zero negative impact by 2020.
Patagonia	To build the best product, cause no unnecessary harm, use business to inspire and implement solutions to the environmental crisis.
Templestowe College	To help students take control of their own learning.
Etsy	Reimagining commerce in ways that build a more fulfilling and lasting world.
Hitnet	Co-creating knowledge to transforms lives.
Atlassian	To unleash the power in every team.
Get Up	Giving everyday Australians the chance to make extraordinary impact – online, across the airwaves and in the streets.
1 Million Women	Building a movement of strong, inspirational women and girls acting on climate change through the way we live.

Using this framework, have a play with your own personal purpose statement.

You may wish to review your notes from The Purpose Questions in part 2 before you do this.

Organise a team meeting and share the model and theory with your team at an organisational level.

If you have a current purpose statement, map it out against this framework. Does it work? Is it meaningful? Can you tell stories to support the statement? Is it enacted? How inspiring is it for you all to turn up to work each day? (Score 1-10: 1 being totally unmotivated, 10 being fully-motivated.)

Is there anything that needs to be done to review/change your purpose statement?

SAFETYCULTURE'S STORY

" The life purpose of the true social entrepreneur is to change the world. ""
- Bill Drayton

Luke Anear is the founder of SafetyCulture, the company behind the world's best workplace safety inspection app, iAuditor. The app is used by many of the world's largest companies and the company is now set to expand exponentially thanks to a further $30 million dollars in venture capital funding.

"Every 15 seconds someone dies from a workplace incident or illness and 153 people are injured globally. That's 6300 people each day," says Luke. "I'm driven by a deep desire to eliminate workplace tragedies by scaling iAuditor's use and impact."

SafetyCulture's mission [purpose] is: 'making safety available to every worker in the world'.

"It gives our people a reason to turn up to work every day. They know they're not just building great apps, that they're actually saving lives," claims Luke. "Recently I had a new engineer say to me that he didn't really understand why we were building this particular extra feature on iAuditor, and that terrified me, so I sent a team of 12 people to Bangladesh to talk to victims of workplace accidents so they could witness the impact of their work first hand."

"Our next team trip is to Nepal in May and then Chile in August. As well as showing our people why their work is so vital, we'll tell the stories of the major workplace incidents that have happened in these countries. It's the best way to show the true cost of unsafe workplaces and their dire consequences. It's how I keep our people connected to our reason for existence and the foundation of company culture. When they hear the words of the survivors of workplace accidents, they get deeply connected at an emotional level – it changes their lives and how they show up at work."

Recently the company screened the movie *Deepwater Horizon* for all their people. It's the story of BPs disastrous oil rig spill off the Gulf of Mexico in 2010 where 11 people went missing and were never found. The company flew in one of the survivors and after the movie was screened, he walked onto the stage and shared his story. "The impact on our people was profound," says Luke.

SafetyCulture's purpose statement is precise, practical and meaningful and it follows all the ingredients of the framework: a verb (making); what/intention (safety available to); and a beneficiary (every worker in the world).

This is a powerful statement and meaningful for all stakeholders beyond employees (which is essential to make any purpose a truly collective purpose). It's meaningful for the clients who buy and use the app and their employees and their families who want to know their loved ones are safe at work.

Compare this to a purpose statement I recently noticed for a global public institution 'to create a better future today'. There are many purpose statements in the market similar to this. To me, it's a nebulous and purposeless purpose statement. As an employee, I'd be asking a few questions. What does this actually mean? What do you want me to do? How do I take ownership of this?

What might your company learn from SafetyCulture's story?

 Watch the SafetyCulture Bangladesh story on The Slow School of Business YouTube channel.

TELSTRA'S STORY

> " *Customers will never love a company until*
> *employees love it first.* "
> - Simon Sinek

Some time ago I delivered a talk on the topic of purpose to about 200 employees of Telstra, Australia's largest telecommunications company.

Towards the end of the talk I shared Telstra's company purpose statement with them. I had planned to ask the audience to tell me their purpose but decided against it to save any potential embarrassment in case no one knew it. (9 times of out 10, I find that employees don't actually know the company purpose, which of course, renders it superfluous.)

Telstra's purpose is, 'to create a brilliant connected future for everyone.'

Regardless of your views on Telstra and whether you believe the purpose promise matches the purpose experience, I truly believe it's a powerful purpose statement with enormous potential. It fits beautifully with the preceding framework and there's strength behind every word. Create. Brilliant. Connected. Future. Everyone.

I shared with the audience that, no doubt, they're attending to this purpose from a technical and technological perspective and at a rational and functional level. I then suggested that their greatest challenge and opportunity lies in actually humanising their purpose and bringing that word 'connected' to life for the benefit of absolutely 'everyone'.

I shared that as humans, every single one of us is hardwired for connection, that we all crave a sense of belonging and of feeling valued. I suggested that the people of Telstra not only had the technological power to bring their purpose to life, but the heart-centred human power too - if they were just willing to own it. I told them that the company *why* was not the sole responsibility of their manager or the executive team to deliver on, and that it was up to each of them to take responsibility for it.

If I'd had the foresight, I would have led a short meditation and asked them to drop that purpose statement right into their heart. I would have asked them to feel what their daily work would be like if they were humanising this purpose. I'd have slowly gone through each of the words in the statement and asked them to consider their human potential. I would have asked them what really matters to them in life and work and what contribution they wish to make beyond the day-to-day functions of their job. And there may have been tears (probably on my part too), but hey, that's where the magic happens.

In my opinion, Telstra's purpose statement deserves deep reverence and commitment. It's a purpose that all employees could grab hold of, take personal ownership of and make their own - which is why a company even bothers having a higher purpose in the first place.

I believe it would be a great shame for Telstra to mess with its purpose. While I'm not privy to the numerous culture/change/leadership programs they must be spending millions on right now, one thing is for sure, their company purpose should be the fundamental foundation on which every initiative hangs. It's the ultimate way to create a healthy culture and bring life back to work.

THE PURPOSE HEALTH-CHECK

 Never go to a doctor whose office plants have died.
- Erma Bombeck

When you go the doctor for a check-up, the first thing she'll check is your heart and its capacity to keep ticking and keep you alive. And it's the same with your company purpose, the heart of your company. Your purpose requires a regular check-up and testing for its relevance and direction as your company and the environment you operate in, evolves. It can and should change, not too often or just when a new CEO takes over the helm, but when it feels like it's not adequately serving or motivating your people and other stakeholders.

And it deserves more than a cursory conversation during an annual strategy day with the leadership team. It requires deep, company-wide attention.

There are numerous online staff engagement tools and surveys you can customise to measure purpose. These are ideal for gathering the base intelligence required to understand the gap between where you are now and where you need to be and to determine the best approach to closing the gap with *Purpose Projects*.

Before doing a purpose health-check, be sure to host a 'purpose' education session with your staff to give them the essential context before the detailed content. They need to be engaged in what purpose means, why it's important and its place in driving vision, mission and values. It would be useful to share the models and contents of this book as the precursor to your health-check.

> Your purpose requires a regular check-up and testing for its relevance and direction as your company and the environment you operate in, evolves.

Once the education piece is done, you can use a combination of online tools and interviews with people to assess just what the purpose gap might be in the organisation. This list of questions will help you assess the gap.

1. Do you think we need purpose as a company? If so, why? If not, why not?

2. Do we have a company purpose that you are aware of?

3. If so, what is our purpose? Please state.

4. What does our purpose actually mean to you?

5. How motivated and inspired are you by our purpose? (Score 1-5: 1 being 'not at all', 5 being 'totally')

6. How well does our company live by this purpose? (Score 1-5: 1 being 'not at all' to 5 being 'absolutely always'.)

7. Do our suppliers/customers/partners/shareholders/other stakeholders know what it is? If so, are they engaged with it?

8. Share a story or example of where our purpose has/has not been demonstrated.

9. Is our purpose still relevant? Does it need updating?

10. If you don't know our purpose or don't believe we have one, what do you think it should be?

11. Do you feel enabled to bring your own purpose/passion to work? (Yes/No, Why/Why not?)

12. If you were to *BYO Purpose* to work, what might that look like for you?

13. Do we balance purpose with profit in our company? Yes/No - give an example.

14. How important to you, is purpose as the driver of our organisation? (Score 1-5: 1 being 'not at all', 5 being 'totally'). Why is it important?

15. What would you like to see the company do to bring more meaning to our workplace? Name one big initiative we could adopt and smaller ideas that could be activated on a daily basis.

Does your company purpose need a health-check?

If so, how might you use these questions to engage your team on purpose?

What can you do to test the company purpose overall?

What action will you take now?

THE PURPOSE EFFECT

It takes but one person, one moment, one conviction, to start a ripple of change.
- Donna Brazille

A clearly stated company purpose has the potential to create a ripple effect across your enterprise. Any *Purpose Activist* who is truly connected to the purpose (and their own) will be constantly dropping the pebble of purpose into their presentations, conversations and most importantly, their deeds. That's how movements are started and cultures are healed. It becomes a case of "I want what he's having. How can I get plugged into our/my purpose too?"

As the glue of the organisation, an activated purpose can make teams more effective and connect people across silos. Purpose forms the foundation on which strategy is created, meetings are held and decisions are made. "Is this decision in line with our highest purpose?" should be the common question on everyone's lips in all interactions.

Purpose can become the central aspect of every part of your company operations. It affects the way you market your company, the way you recruit, the way you communicate with customers and the way you sell. It directs the products you build and bring to market, the loyalty of your employees, your customers and your suppliers. It even has an effect on your industry and your competition and the communities within which you operate.

One of the most powerful ways to bring purpose to life, is through storytelling. Stories have the power to

A clearly stated company purpose has the potential to create a ripple effect across your enterprise.

change dry, data-driven presentations and communications into heart-driven, storytelling pow-wows that ignite and inspire people to action.

The 'purpose effect' is powerful. That's why it's worth investing in at all levels of your organisation. And the best thing is, you can start today, right where you are with all that you have right now. (Yes, I know I keep repeating myself!)

Who are the specific people in various departments across your company (or outside your company) who would be interested in having a purpose conversation with you?

How will you reach out to them and meet with them to get the purpose ripple effect happening? What would be the format and purpose of your catch up/meeting?

When will you do it?

THE MANIFESTO

> *All life is the manifestation of the spirit, a manifestation of love.*
> - Morihei Ueshiba

A great way to start the purpose ripple effect is through producing your own manifesto. A manifesto is a public declaration of how you behave every day. It provides a heart-felt way to communicate your purpose, vision, mission and values.

A manifesto is like a guiding philosophy. It guides what you think, feel and do to fulfil your higher purpose. My favourite personal manifesto is the famous *Holstee Manifesto* which is not only a written word declaration for each of us to live by, but also a very beautiful video.

At an enterprise level, lululemon, the yoga and sportswear company, has a wonderful manifesto. It's a collection of bold thoughts that ignite conversations while communicating their company culture to their community. It's the basis of the company strategy, employee engagement and their branding, marketing and community building activities. Lululemon is more than a company. It's a movement! I've yet to meet a woman who does not absolutely love lululemon, not just for its products but for everything it stands for as a company.

Manifestos can be created for any person, subject, enterprise or even a team within a large enterprise. I live by a personal manifesto that I wrote about three years ago and also have a *Marketing Manifesto* and a *Learning Manifesto* for *Slow School*.

Manifestos can guide life partnerships, parents and families. Brené Brown has written a beautiful parenting manifesto that she and her husband live by. What a wonderful experience for a couple or family to develop a manifesto together that becomes the guide for how they live, love, work and play together.

You can use the following model to start crafting your own manifesto. Start by considering the things you need to think, feel and do to bring purpose, vision, mission and values to life. It can be helpful to revisit your 'I believe…' statements from your journaling too. Start broad and produce as many statements and words as possible before narrowing it down. There are then many ways it can be communicated whether that's through the written word, spoken word, audio, video or printed posters and handbooks. Then, of course, words must become deeds, lest the manifesto becomes meaningless.

Manifestos are magnificent! They've guided me many times in the making of decisions and in helping me communicate my philosophies and purpose.

Time to have some fun working on a manifesto of your choice. Your own personal one? A family one? A team one? Once you've chosen the subject of your manifesto, check out the ones I've mentioned here. Review the journal pages where you answered The Purpose Questions for some inspiration.

The Manifesto

What do we need to Think, Feel, Do to fulfill our Purpose, Vision, Mission & Values?

Think - HEAD

Feel - HEART

Do - ACTION

IT'S UP TO YOU

"You must take personal responsibility. You cannot change the circumstances, the seasons, or the wind, but you can change yourself. That is something you have charge of."
- Jim Rohn

I'm a firm believer that it's everyone's responsibility to unearth and activate purpose in an organisation, to become a *Purpose Activist*, not just the appointed leaders. So, I've attempted to provide you with a range of philosophies and tools to help you do this, regardless of your standing in the company. The tools are designed as thought-starters and heart-starters, a way for you to ignite the purpose conversation with your peers and to see where it takes you.

Even if the company you work for lacks a higher purpose than profit and is unwilling to go on the purpose journey, I still challenge you to step into your full power and bring your own purpose to work. I encourage you to educate yourself on the topic, to watch videos, read the books I've suggested and to share what you learn with others.

But mostly I encourage you to give things a go, to try things out and test this purpose thing for yourself through your own *Purpose Project* (part 5). The path to finding your work purpose, whether you're a student, a solo business owner or an employee of a multi-national company lies in doing not mere dreaming.

> Even if the company you work for lacks a higher purpose than profit and is unwilling to go on the purpose journey, I still challenge you to step into your full power and bring your own purpose to work.

Before moving onto the next section of this book, take an hour for yourself to do a stocktake on where you are at right now.

Review your journal and reflect on any patterns, signs, ideas that are coming up that might become a potential project.

Review your *Statement of Intention*. How are you going with it? Are you on track? Does it need to be reviewed, revised, reset? If so, do this and reset your commitment to keep doing this work.

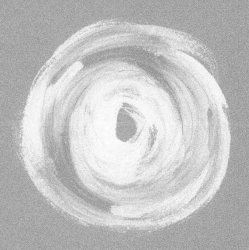

PART 4

THE 12 PRACTICES OF
PURPOSE

INTRODUCING THE 12 PRACTICES

Everything is practice.
- Pele

If we're not evolving personally (physically, spiritually, emotionally and mentally) we'll find it impossible to evolve professionally and in our work life. We'll miss the nuances, the signs, the opportunities that might lead us in a new direction towards meaningful work.

Our latent talents and passions are most often rediscovered when we least expect it and in places of deep reverence: on the dance floor, in nature, in a long hot bath, in your journal, while listening to music, in the ocean, reading poetry, in an unfamiliar town or country, in conversation with a stranger on a train.

In other words, we discover our passion in experiences outside our day-to-day routines. We practise new ways of being and behaving in our daily lives, and then we listen and take notice. We connect with the parts of ourselves that have been asleep: our heart, our spirit, our body and in ways we've never connected before. That's how we heal ourselves and make change happen.

Over the years, I've adopted a number of new behaviours that have led me to my calling. Until now, I never had a name for them and I was practising them unintentionally. It's only as I've written this book that I've become aware of how integral they've been. And as I continue to evolve, they've become richer and more rewarding.

For each practice, I'll share my own anecdotes to give you context on how I've used them and also the stories of others who are on their path to meaningful work. My aim is to show you how 'ordinary' people make 'extraordinary' shifts in their lives and how they keep it real and doable.

That word 'practise' is a verb, a doing word. To find the work you really want to be doing in the world, you must become a 'practitioner of purpose'. Through practice we make progress, not perfection. Through practice we gain clarity.

Some of the practices and accompanying activities will resonate more than others; however, do them all, no matter how well you think you're doing at each one. Don't judge them or question them, just do them. You may be surprised at what comes up and what you uncover. Have a mind that is open to everything and closed to nothing. I also suggest repeating the activities for the practices where you're most stuck or resistant.

You might focus on one practice per week or one per month depending on how much work you feel you need to do. Develop a plan that works for you and block out time in your diary to commit to the practices. You can also work with the support system and people that you've hopefully created by now - a coach, a purpose buddy or your mastermind group.

Before you get started, it might be useful to review your *Statement of Intention* from part 1 of this book to take a quick peak at how you're going.

That word 'practise' is a verb, a doing word. To find the work you really want to be doing in the world, you must become a 'practitioner of purpose'. Through practice we make progress, not perfection. Through practice we gain clarity.

PRACTICE 1
THE PRACTICE OF SURRENDERING

> *Always say 'yes' to the present moment.*
> *Surrender to what is. Say 'yes' to life - and see*
> *how life suddenly starts working for you rather*
> *than against you.*
> - Eckhart Tolle

Give in. Give up. Submit. Throw in the towel. Lay down your arms. Raise the white flag. These may be just some of the terms that come to mind when you read that word 'surrender'. Many of us associate the word surrender with being at war, an event where we suffer crippling defeat at the hands of our enemies.

Perhaps you feel that you're always at war? You're at war with another person or some external circumstance beyond your control. You're at war with your boss, a family member, a friend or the dominant culture. (Many of us feel at war with the dominant culture, by the way, but we haven't yet recognised it or surrendered to it.) The biggest battle we face, however, is not the battle with others, it's the battle we face with ourselves.

If we're not surrendering, we're fighting. We're in a perpetual state of surrender or victory as we hold on tight to the rails of our personal ladder of success (whatever our own version of success is).

It's an exhausting existence.

Surrendering, however, is the first step on the path to pursuing your life's work. We must surrender to the externalities of our life and we must surrender to our internalities – to ourselves. The act of surrendering is painful yet essential. You acknowledge and accept your work/life situation as it is right now. It's neither good nor bad. It just is. You don't judge or criticise it. You surrender to your emotions, your discomfort, your uncertainty and your insecurity.

So how do you do this? Firstly, you start where you are. You do not run away from the discomfort, push it away or numb your feelings with shopping, social media, alcohol, drugs, over-working, busyness or whatever other substance you use to distance yourself from yourself. You say 'yes' to what is happening right now. You don't give up or give in. That's called helplessness. You acknowledge it and accept it.

And you do this by relinquishing control. Control is actually the opposite of surrender, not victory. Control keeps us tight, locked up and closed to the possibilities. When you attempt to control every activity, every day, every relationship, every situation in your life, you become closed down to life. You are so focused on the victory, there's no joy in the game itself.

If you know *what* you're aiming for and *why* you want it, then you won't be so worried about *how* it comes about. When you hold the *how* loosely, magic happens. Control is the result of being focused on the *how* without knowing the *what* or the *why*. It's like being so focused on scaling to the top of the ladder that you don't even realise the ladder is placed against the wrong wall.

When you give up control, you enter a state of surrender.

The famous Serenity Prayer says, "God grant me the serenity to accept the things I cannot change, the courage to change the things I can and the wisdom to know the difference". You gracefully and calmly accept the things that you cannot change and you set an intention to gently work on the things that you can change. You practise surrendering each day. You build up your capacity to surrender until one day you find yourself at a turning point. You become clear-minded enough to make a choice that will change your trajectory.

Control is the result of being focused on the how without knowing the *what* or the *why*. It's like being so focused on scaling to the top of the ladder that you don't even realise the ladder is placed against the wrong wall.

In surrender mode, you're calm, peaceful, gently smiling, deeply breathing, meditating, reflective, present. You're conscious. You're in a state of grace. You're ready to hand it over. You hand it over to a higher power, nature, the universe, God, a trusted friend, a counsellor or a 12-step group, whichever will give you the support you need. What is it that you need to hand over?

Surrender means to stop fighting with others and yourself, to completely accept what is, to have faith that you're right where you're meant to be, right now. Surrendering is the ultimate act of self-love.

You must first surrender to what is, if you're to create the work-life you desire.

In my travel memoir *Unstuck in Provence*, I start at the exact moment I awoke on the morning of the 17th May to make a decision to start over again. I began the book at my turning point, but what I didn't write about was the months of surrendering I went through to get me to that point.

There were many low periods as I became increasingly aware I was not leading the life I'd hoped for, nor doing work I loved any more. For example, one day I was in the midst of a marketing strategy session with a client and the conversation turned to the minutiae of their website. I had a sudden feeling I was out of integrity, that this was not meaningful work for me anymore.

There were many, many instances like this, until one day I chose to stop 'being a marketer'. I let go of my attachment to my professional moniker - a supreme act of surrender. I was no longer a 'marketer', I just used to practise marketing and now I was a free-agent. (Just as you are not a lawyer, you just happen to practise law or whatever profession you may be in.)

Through the support of my counsellor and my willingness to be honest with myself, I surrendered to everything – my old work life and a number of other things that were keeping me stuck too.

Each day, each week, each month, I surrendered just a little bit more. This surrendering was necessary to get me to my turning

Surrendering enabled me to make that choice through love rather than fear. (Fear is never a good basis on which to make profound life choices.)

point so I could make the best choices for myself and Billy. Surrendering enabled me to make that choice through love rather than fear. (Fear is never a good basis on which to make profound life choices.)

MATT'S STORY

In 2001, Matt Perfect graduated from his Bachelor of Economics at Cardiff Business School in the UK. After 13 years as a hard-working, well-respected management consultant and procurement professional, he made the decision to end his corporate career and start his own business.

In the previous couple of years, he'd been starting to have a series of pinpricks to the conscience about his work and profession. He was feeling increasingly out of place with the profit-driven world of procurement that measured its success solely through its ability to cut costs and he had a growing sense of dissatisfaction with his day-to-day work.

Then one evening as he was reading a story to his 3-year-old daughter, she asked, "Daddy, what do you do at work all day?" "What followed was an uncomfortable conversation as I tried to sell the value of my work to her", says Matt. "I couldn't explain to her what I did with any real sense of pride or purpose, and she clearly wasn't buying my answer." From that moment, Matt surrendered a little more each day to the realisation that he wasn't personally fulfilled by his work or the profession. He also realised that he'd always bought into the dominant capitalist narrative that business existed to make a profit and that a career was about making money, while doing good was what you did outside of work. He realised that this premise was fundamentally flawed and that it was possible to do good and make money simultaneously.

This experience set him on a whole new path. He quit his job to start a business. He got curious and he took action. He became passionate about helping companies make conscious choices on their spending and procurement so that they'd have a positive impact on humanity and the environment. He found his conscious business tribes at *Slow School* and *Conscious Capitalism*. He started speaking on the topic of impact spending and writing articles on it. He stepped up to become a cause-leader in his industry.

Today the doors are starting to open in a whole new direction for Matt. "Since starting my business, I've done a lot of work to gain clarity on my purpose, beliefs and values. I've partnered with a handful of organisations where I have strong values alignment with the founders and had quite a few other financially lucrative opportunities put in front of me that I've declined. Having clarity of purpose has helped me make wise choices around what I say 'yes' to and what I say 'no' to."

"But best of all," says Matt, "I can now proudly share with my daughter what I believe in and what I do at work all day. I feel that I'm setting a great example for my kids." Matt's advice to others? "Surrender first to the discomfort and understand that you don't have to have the answer right away. Just recognise where you are right now and then follow your curiosity, go exploring and start experimenting."

 Watch Matt Perfect's talk on The Slow School of Business YouTube channel.

TIME TO PRACTISE

Meditation & Reflection	Find a quiet spot where you'll be uninterrupted or go for a silent walk to reflect on the following questions. Do this exercise for at least 30 minutes while breathing fully into it. Try to drop into your body and your heart as much as possible and feel the answers and not over-think it.
	What are the things in your life that you have the power to change that are holding you back from reaching your highest potential? Get really specific. Why, and how, are they holding you back? What is the absolute truth of the impact they're having on you? What are the deepest emotions they evoke in you? Where do you feel them in your body and heart (feel the sensations)? What might your daily life feel like if you were to fully surrender these things? What can you do right now to take the first step towards surrendering? Do you need support for this? If so, how will you get it, where will you get it and who will you seek it from? How will fully surrendering to these things help you reach your highest potential?
	(Note: These things can be both small and large and they might be situations or people. For example, not getting enough sleep, addiction to social media, over-consumption of alcohol, a heartless boss, a partner who is unsupportive, financial stress. They are things or circumstances you have the power to change.)
Journaling Exercise	Now write for 30 minutes on the following:
	1. Journal about all the answers to the questions in your meditation and reflection exercise.
	2. What is your current state/capacity for surrender? (Rank 1-10: 1 being totally blocked/stuck and unable to surrender, 10 being able to enter a full state of daily surrender)
	3. What would you like your state/capacity for surrender to be? (Rank 1-10 as above)
	4. What is the gap? Identify how large the gap is between questions 2 and 3 to determine how much of a priority this practice is.
	5. Set an intention for this practice.
	"I will practise surrendering by..." "I will know when I have fulfilled this intention when..."
Daily Practice	Identify one firm practice you will adopt in order to surrender more each day. What is it? How will you ensure you undertake this daily practice?
Big Action	Identify one big thing you will surrender this week.
	What is it? When and how will you do it?

PRACTICE 2
THE PRACTICE OF FINDING COURAGE

Life shrinks or expands in proportion to one's courage.
- Anaïs Nin

If I could only choose one practice out of the whole 12 in this book, courage would be it! Maya Angelou summed up why, in this one statement, "Courage is the most important of all the virtues, because without courage you can't practice any other virtue consistently. You can practice any virtue erratically, but nothing consistently without courage."

Courage is the gateway to consciousness, to freedom and fulfilling your life's work. Courage is the ability to do something that frightens you and that stretches your capability and capacity to grow. Without it, you'll not take the first step towards your calling.

The *Top 5 Five Regrets of the Dying*, is a book by Bronnie Ware, a palliative care nurse who cared for many people in their last days before dying. Through her many conversations with them, she discovered their number one regret was not having the courage to live a life true to themselves, instead of the life others expected of them. It's pretty confronting to realise that for the vast majority of us, extrinsic forces are more powerful in dictating our life direction than our own natural intrinsic forces.

(Incidentally the other top four regrets were: I wish I hadn't worked so hard; I wish I'd had the courage to

> Courage is the gateway to consciousness, to freedom and fulfilling your life's work. Courage is the ability to do something that frightens you and that stretches your capability and capacity to grow. Without it, you'll not take the first step towards your calling.

express my feelings; I wish I'd stayed in touch with my friends; I wish that I'd let myself be happier.)

It takes courage to not live your life according to family, societal and institutional rules and to swim against the tide of conformity. But if you don't do this, you can't ultimately make the highest and most positive contribution. You won't become wicked examples for your kids and for future generations. At worst, you'll die having lived an unfulfilled life.

Courage is not about taking reckless risks or radically overhauling every aspect of your life at once. Courage is also not something you just turn on when you have big decisions to make. Finding courage is a daily practice to adopt like brushing your teeth. It's about upping your overall 'courage factor' in small and big ways.

You were born with a courage factor of 10 (1 = totally uncourageous and 10 = truly courageous). When you were young you showed great acts of courage and you were 100% true to yourself. You sang, painted, danced and climbed trees and you didn't care what others thought. You didn't even know you were being courageous. Courageousness was your natural state. As you grew up, perhaps your courage factor became diminished? Somewhere along the line you became more concerned with pleasing others, avoiding conflict and taking the preordained path. Maybe over time, your courage factor dropped down to a 3 or 4?

Upping your overall courage factor requires consistency. Each day you do something that scares you and makes you uncomfortable and that takes you closer to your calling.

You book those singing lessons you've promised yourself for years. You tenaciously keep contacting the HR department of that company you really want to work for. You address the elephant in the room at your team meeting and face the possible consequences. You invite that stranger you met on the train out for coffee. You say sorry to someone you've wronged. You're the first to say, 'I love you'. You share your deepest vulnerabilities with your co-workers. You end that unhealthy relationship

Upping your overall courage factor requires consistency. Each day you do something that scares you and makes you uncomfortable and that takes you closer to your calling.

with your long-standing nemesis – whether that's a person or a thing, such as an addiction to alcohol.

Courage is about giving a firm 'no', when in the past you might've said 'yes' to someone to please them or to something that keeps you stuck, yet perversely comfortable. It's also about giving a firm 'yes' to those people and things you just know will be good for you that you've never had the gumption for.

The greatest acts of courage do not cost you anything. They simply involve the release of your own limited thinking, your fear of the unknown and the fear of what others will think.

Courage is about saying NO to what you don't want and YES to what you do. It's about asking for what you desire, unapologetically and wholeheartedly without attachment to the outcome.

Courage is the sister of creativity (another practice in this book). It takes great courage to unleash your innate creativity. If you think about your life journey so far, you'll see that all the events that stand out and that brought you the most joy, required both courage and creativity.

Releasing my own work into the world requires constant flexing of my courage muscle. Obviously it's open to public criticism. As I've got older and bolder in my writing, I've opened myself up to the possibility of even more criticism. At the same time, I care less and less for others' opinions. That's what increasing your courage factor does. It makes you less susceptible to others' judgements and even more committed to your work. What you think of me, and my work, is actually none of my business!

My first two books were quite conservative. They were in my pre-France days when I hadn't started on the purpose journey. They required some courage to release because they were my inaugural launch into authorship but not as much courage as my 2012 e-book, *The Conscious Marketing Revolution* (the precursor to the full book, *Conscious Marketing*).

In this book, I accused us all of being unconscious binge marketers declaring most marketing and advertising to be rubbish and contributing to the destruction of humanity. On the verge of releasing it to my email list, I was sure I was about to commit career suicide and I lacked the courage to hit send. So instead of bailing, I sought the wise counsel of my sister, Angela. "Caz," she said, "dead fish go with the flow." There was no way I was going to be a dead fish, so ten minutes later the book was released. My courage factor was upped with one simple email.

Then in 2013, my courage was tested yet again. The manuscript for *Unstuck in Provence* had remained unpublished for three years. I just couldn't find the nerve to let others read something so excruciatingly private and I was concerned about the potential impact on Billy and my ex-husband. I recall vividly how nervous I was the day I handed Billy the manuscript for his review and consent to publish. I also recall the two glasses of wine it took before I could hit send on the email to my ex-husband with the manuscript for his consent too. Wine, when consumed wisely, really ups the courage factor!

Courage is my constant companion in my writing. Each word leads to a page of words, which leads to a chapter, which leads to a book, which leads to another book. What do you need the companionship of courage for?

BILLY'S STORY

From the age of three, Billy was always dressing up, singing, dancing and acting. One minute he was Harry Potter, the next he was Woody from Toy Story and the next Spiderman. He was a natural performer always staging an impromptu production for any visitor to the house. In his later years in primary school he started to show a real aptitude for acting and dancing and it seemed like he might even pursue a vocation in the performing arts.

Then just as he started high school at the age of 12, he suddenly decided that all the singing and acting stuff was not for him and he wanted to give it up. I was saddened and perplexed as to how he could give away something that he so clearly loved. My attempts to investigate his decision turned up nothing and as I'm no Tiger Mother, I reluctantly accepted his decision. I came to understand, however, that while it was his choice, it was made in an attempt to fit in with the dominant sports culture at school (sport being something he had little interest in).

Some four years later, Billy came home one day to announce that he'd decided to study drama for his last two years of high school. It was music to my ears. While he didn't participate in any of the school's excellent productions or get actively involved in any theatre or music groups, behind the scenes he was quietly having private singing lessons. It seemed like he was waiting to escape the confines of the school ground to find the courage to publicly reveal his true creative talents.

While he received an excellent education in the context of what's on offer in the world of education today, I sometimes feel sad that he felt unable to embrace his crazy, talented, arty side in the public domain.

Now out of school and at university doing an Arts degree and living in a residential college, Billy is flourishing. He's performed in his first ever musical, Rent, and in the inter-college Battle of the Bands as well as taken leadership roles at college. He's also co-founded a business that sells suits online to fellow students. It's a purpose-driven business with the desire to empower students and LGBTQI youth as they wear high-quality affordable suits that are hand-made by a third-generation tailoring family from Udaipur in India. He's also working part-time at a youth charity, Oak Tree.

Whether Billy pursues a vocation in the arts, in business or in the corporate world (or all three at once), is unimportant right now. I love that he's taking on all these *Purpose Projects* to discover his passions and that he's being 100% true to himself.

What's also interesting is that his potential future calling is being explored by tapping into his past. What he loved so much at age three is again being loved and embraced at age 19!

If I were to apply the courage factor to Billy's life as it is now, I'd say he's gone from a 3 to a 10 in the space of a year. He's living a wholehearted life that is 100% true to him. What one thing could you unearth from your past to truly 'up' your courage factor?

TIME TO PRACTISE

Meditation & Reflection	Find a quiet spot where you'll be uninterrupted or go for a silent walk to reflect on the following questions. Do this exercise for at least 30 minutes while breathing fully into it. Try to drop into your body and your heart as much as possible and feel the answers and not over-think it.
	Are you living a life that is true to you? Are you being authentically you?
	If yes, how? If not, how not? In what areas of your life do you require more courage? What would a life of courage look like for you?
	Who are the people (those you know and those you don't) you admire that exhibit great courage? What is it about their courage that inspires you? What leaf could you take out of their book? What courageous conversations do you need to have and with whom? What action could you take to be more courageous? How will courage help you to reach your highest potential?
Journaling Exercise	Now write for 30 minutes on the following:
	1. Journal about all the answers to the questions in your meditation and reflection exercise.
	2. What is your current overall courage factor? (Rank 1-10: 1 being totally uncourageous, 10 being totally courageous)
	3. What would you like your overall courage factor to be? (Rank 1-10 as above)
	4. What is the gap? Identify how large the gap is between questions 2 and 3 to determine how much of a priority this practice is.
	5. Set an intention for this practice. "I will practise finding courage by..." "I will know when I have fulfilled this intention when..."
Daily Practice	Identify one firm daily practice you will adopt in order to be more courageous. What is it? How will you ensure you undertake this daily practice?
Big Action	Identify one big courageous thing you will do this week. What is it? When and how will you do it?

PRACTICE 3
THE PRACTICE OF SELF-CARE

*Our bodies are our gardens to which
our wills are gardeners.*
- William Shakespeare

Self-care is care provided 'for you, by you'. It's about identifying and understanding your own physical, mental, spiritual and emotional needs and taking steps to meet them. It's about being kind to yourself and doing activities that nurture you. And a big part of self-care is all about doing work you really care for!

On another point, the reason many of us are in unhealthy or unsatisfying relationships is because we're care-taking practitioners instead of self-care practitioners. We're so frantic trying to put the oxygen mask on other people that we forget to put on our own oxygen mask first.

So, let's get physical and start with your body.

Americans spend $400 billion a year on fast food and junk food and a further $60 billion a year on weight-loss products. What's wrong with this picture? The only ones winning in this toxic weight-gain and weight-loss war, are the diet and the junk food companies. Their sole purpose is to turn your weight-pain into their wealth-gain.

So, it's time to change this picture. Good food is your medicine. It gives you the energy and clarity you need to make good choices. You don't need a special diet or pill to change what you eat. You just need the know-how, the willpower and a reason. Perhaps that reason is the possibility of reaching your most magnificent human potential?

I also recommend radically reducing (or eliminating) other substances like alcohol, caffeine, prescribed drugs and illegal drugs. In Australia, 15 people die each day from alcohol-related illnesses, yet still our binge-drinking culture is socially acceptable and even admired! Try replacing wine with water for a few months – you might just never go back.

What you put in your body completely changes what your body (and mind) can do!

If the first act of self-care is to put good fuel in your body, the second act is to move your body. We should all stop 'exercising' (much like dieting), striving for that six-pack or thigh-gap, and simply start moving. Variety is the spice of life. Try dancing, swimming, yoga, tai chi, bike riding, bush walking, kick boxing, team sports or sailing. Do one fun activity every day. Just move your body and love your body.

And now let's discuss emotional self-care – the ability to recognise, accept and deal with your emotions in a healthy way. There are hundreds of emotions to experience in any given day: anger, fear, sadness, joy, disgust, trust, happiness, shame, vulnerability, envy, love, loneliness, lust and hate.

Popular culture pedals the pursuit of 'happiness' as though it's the holy grail of a good life. While happiness is wonderful, all emotions are valid and essential. Your goal is to have a whole-hearted life with a full-spectrum of emotions, including the painful ones. Sadness, anger and fear are potent catalysts for pursuing your purpose, but only if they're fully felt. Most addictions are the result of fleeing from painful emotions instead of feeling right into them and using them as the servant of growth.

So how do you practise emotional self-care? Go back to practice 1 and 2, then find a counsellor, therapist or a 12-step program (not a GP who will simply prescribe a pill for your pain). (12-step programs which deal with a range of addictions, are based on the foundations of Alcoholics Anonymous and have saved millions of people from destructive addictions.) Notice your emotions. Accept them. Get curious. Journal about them. Share them with a trusted friend. Take responsibility for your own emotions and stop blaming others for them.

> What you put in your body completely changes what your body (and mind) can do!

Embrace every emotion on your emotional paint palette, because it's from here that you'll paint your masterpiece.

And now to spiritual self-care, the bed-partner of physical and emotional self-care. Spiritual self-care is your ability to maintain inner peace for your body and soul through connecting to a higher power: God, Krishna, Buddha, The Universe, Spirit or Mother Earth.

Your spirit is everywhere, around you and within you. Your spirit is at play when you notice serendipity or synchronicity happening. You think of someone you haven't spoken to for years and all of a sudden they're calling you. You take a bushwalk and feel a complete sense of oneness with the trees and the earth beneath. You watch a crimson sunset settle over the city skyline and are moved to tears. You hear a piece of music that makes your body pulse and your heart burst open. You feel a sense of flow in your work.

The practice of spiritual self-care requires a commitment to act daily: to pray, meditate, journal, listen to music, sit in nature and breathe deeply. It requires you to follow your intuition and to bring your soul into alignment with your highest truth.

And finally, mental self-care - the ability to recognise, accept and manage your thoughts so you can channel them into positive behaviour in alignment with your intentions. What we think, we become. I've touched on this subject throughout this book and I dig far deeper on it in Practice 6: The Practice of Becoming Conscious.

This year, the practice of physical self-care has been at the top of my 12 practices. One of my three major intentions for 2017 is to be the fittest and healthiest I've ever been. That's a pretty big intention yet one that's really starting to come to fruition. What fuelled this intention was the deepest realisation that I must be at peak health and fitness if I'm going to have the power and presence required to deliver on my work purpose.

So, I made some big shifts in my everyday life that has involved a change in how much, and when, I consume alcohol, the elimination of

> Embrace every emotion on your emotional paint palette, because it's from here that you'll paint your masterpiece.

meat, fats and sugars and the adoption of a wonderful 'body moving' regime that includes dancing, yoga, walking, bike riding and swimming.

It's been an evolution rather than a revolution as I take small steps and make adjustments each day and week. On a few occasions, I've seriously slipped up, the details of which I won't be sharing here! This is where it helps to have a good laugh and a sense of self-acceptance. Self-care and self-acceptance are great bed-partners. It's not our aim to be perfect. It's our aim to adopt consistency in our self-care practices so that we can be our best selves and, therefore, do our best work.

KATRINA'S STORY

When I first met Katrina Edwards, she was in a very unhappy place with regard to her work life. She'd been running her three Aligned for Life Pilates studios in Melbourne for 15 years and was finding no joy from it. (Pilates is an exercise system for physical and mental conditioning.) "What was once my passion had turned into a drudgery," shares Katrina. "I was mired in the day-to-day of running the business, constantly tired and putting everyone else's needs first. I was on the verge of giving it all up."

Instead of giving up, she chose to rise up and take the challenge to unearth her *why*. "I'd never thought about my purpose beyond the functional practice of Pilates. I started thinking big about the legacy I wished to leave and came to understand that I'm here to bring physical health and mental wellbeing to people and that Pilates is just one vehicle to do that. I also realised that by changing myself and refocusing on my own health, that others will change too."

Since committing to her *why* everything has expanded for Katrina. "I got brave about expressing myself and my needs. I let go of things that didn't work. I found licensees for the three studios and I got healthy. I reconnected with what I love and why I chose this work in the first place."

Then one day before Christmas, she received a strange email request for a private Pilates training session with two Japanese businessmen from Tokyo. "At first I thought it was spam. I was about to start holidays so I wasn't really that excited about it, but I said yes," says Katrina. "As it turned out they were from a company in Tokyo that teaches yoga and other health programs. They were in Melbourne checking out Pilates teachers and their programs for the purposes of licensing them for the Japanese market."

Three days later, on Christmas eve, Katrina and her husband, Brendan, met with one of the Japanese businessmen to discuss the potential for a partnership. "This is the weird part," says Katrina. "Just two weeks later we were due to fly to Tokyo to set off for a family skiing holiday. I told him we'd meet his team in Tokyo to deliver a proper pitch. He was astounded and said yes immediately. Then I rang Robert, our videographer and asked him to urgently produce some videos with Japanese subtitles featuring my philosophies and methodologies and stories from people I'd helped like Easton Wood of the Western Bulldogs."

Katrina and Brendan pitched to nine businessmen in Tokyo. The meeting went for three hours. "They saw my passion and authenticity and the big picture messages about physical health and wellbeing and the rest is history. I'm now working with them to bring Pilates to the people of Japan to help educate their aging population on how to take charge of their health and wellbeing."

In addition to this, Katrina has reconnected with her passion and talents in ballet and was invited to work part-time at the Australian Ballet School. She also teaches Pilates to some of the players of the Western Bulldogs (AFL) and Melbourne City Football Club (soccer). She's created a portfolio livelihood that she is truly happy with!

"I turned my lack of creativity and enjoyment totally around in 2015 and 2016. I'm thriving again on every level and I love it! I think self-care had a lot to do with this. I put myself first, mentally and physically and was prepared to ask myself the hard questions about what I needed to thrive. As a result, I've gone from having no energy to being an ever-ready battery!" ends Katrina.

 Watch Katrina Edwards talk on The Slow School of Business YouTube channel.

TIME TO PRACTISE

Meditation & Reflection	Find a quiet spot where you'll be uninterrupted, sit or lay down and reflect on the following questions. Do this exercise for at least 30 minutes while breathing fully into it. Try to drop into your body and your heart as much as possible and feel the answers and not over-think it.

Start with a mental scan of your whole body from the tip of your toes to the top of your head.

▶ What sensations are there in each body part?

▶ How do you feel about your physical body overall?

▶ What physical self-care is currently working for you?

▶ What physical self-care is required now for optimal health?

Next place your hand on your heart and breathe deeply into it.

▶ What emotions and feelings are there now?

▶ Identify each emotion and describe it.

▶ What emotional self-care is currently working for you?

▶ What emotional self-care is required now for optimal wellbeing?

Next place your hands on your head and massage your scalp. Check in with your mind.

▶ What thoughts are there?

▶ What limiting thoughts/beliefs are there?

▶ What mental self-care is currently working for you?

▶ What mental self-care is required for optimal wellbeing?

Move your meditation to the world beyond your body. Feel the spirit of nature and the universe all around you. Breathe it in, listen to it, feel it, in and around your body.

▶ What can you feel in the world beyond your body?

▶ What spiritual self-care is currently working for you?

▶ What spiritual self-care is required for optimal wellbeing?

Finally, what would a day in the life of the ultimate in self-care look like for you? What specific self-care activities do you need to practise? What are the priority practices to integrate into your life this year? How will improved self-care help you to reach your highest potential?

Journaling Exercise	Now write for 30 minutes on the following: 1. Journal about all the answers to the questions in your meditation and reflection exercise. 2. What is your current self-care factor? (Rank 1-10: 1 being really very poor, 10 being the ultimate in self-care all round) 3. What would you like your self-care factor to be? (Rank 1-10 as above) 4. What is the gap? Identify how large the gap is between questions 2 and 3 to determine how much of a priority this practice is. 5. Set an intention for this practice. "I will practise more self-care by..." "I will know when I have fulfilled this intention when..."
Daily Practice	Identify at least one firm daily practice you will adopt in order to practise more self-care. What is it? How will you ensure you undertake this daily practice?
Big Action	Identify one big self-care practice/activity you will do this week. What is it? When and how will you do it?

PRACTICE 4
THE PRACTICE OF RE-LEARNING

"We are here to unlearn the teachings of the church, state and our education system.
- Charles Bukowski

We learn many of our deepest and most indelible lessons through our formal schooling systems and institutions and through our parents, teachers, bosses, priests and even celebrities – the people who have the most 'air-time' and that we're most susceptible to. Each has contributed to our learning in both conscious and deeply unconscious ways, and in either helpful or harmful ways.

> Re-learning involves un-learning what's not helpful and then taking control of our own learning through a self-education that's aligned with our passions.

Re-learning is not about rejecting these sources of learning but about practising discernment in choosing what lessons we take on, particularly the ones that may have limited our capacity for reaching our true potential. This involves questioning everything we're being taught and accepting nothing at face value – just like I would expect you to question the theories in this book. Re-learning involves un-learning what's not helpful and then taking control of our own learning through a self-education that's aligned with our passions. We create our own learning curriculum in line with our greatest interests so we may test our future path.

In addition, our world is in information overload thanks to the internet. We have access to it 24/7 and it's available at the click of a few buttons. It's difficult to filter out the information we allow in and determine what is true, important and useful.

Imagine your brain as a cup, full to the brim and overflowing with information

Forget failure. Start learning by experimenting. Be like Thomas.

that's not helpful in the advancement towards your calling. Now tip that cup over and let the information pour out. Tip out only useless lessons and information, not knowledge and wisdom, as they are what remains once you've set the cup straight again. You come back to ground zero. You've unlearnt the unhelpful lessons of old, so you're free to re-learn the new. Now you wisely select the information you refill your cup with as you know that it manifests in your thoughts and behaviours which determines your future. You're very careful about what you read, watch and listen to and the source of that information, whether it's a friend, a book, a class or the media.

You read and listen to unbiased and alternative media sources. You join meetup groups centred on your passions. You seek out alternative business schools like *Slow School, The Change School, ULab* or *The School of Life*. You go to meditation or philosophy classes to expand your mindfulness and beliefs. You seek out the wisdom of a carefully selected coach, mentor or mastermind group. You create your own self-education around your passion through online courses and through reading books and studying the masters of people who are already working in the field of your potential vocation.

And finally, you learn by doing! You get out of your head and you get into action. You roll up your sleeves and have a go. You take up a *Purpose Project* - an experiment. Then you do one more experiment and then another. And then eventually you find that through doing, you're making ground and that just maybe you've found a new path.

In our re-learning endeavours, we must also re-learn the definition of failure. As Thomas Edison said when he invented the light bulb, "I have not failed 10,000 times. I have not failed once. I have succeeded in proving that those 10,000 ways will not work. When I have eliminated the ways that will not work, I will find the way that will work".

Forget failure. Start learning by experimenting. Be like Thomas.

The real turning point in my own re-learning journey was in 2011, when my friend Amy suggested I read the book *Firms of Endearment* by Raj Sisodia. I inhaled the book in about two days. It was the book to change the course of my learning and it led me to getting involved in *Conscious Capitalism*, a global organisation founded by Raj and John Mackey of Whole Foods Market. I began immersing myself in the philosophies behind building a purpose-driven company by reading further conscious business books, watching documentaries and listening to interviews with revolutionary thinkers.

At the same time, I was working at *The Hub* in Melbourne, one of the first ever co-working places in the world. It was (and still is) a place filled with change-makers and entrepreneurs and I was learning a lot just by hanging out in the kitchen and conversing over a cuppa.

Then in May 2012, I saw Raj speaking at the launch of *Conscious Capitalism* in Australia. He made a declaration that marketing could actually be a force for good in the world. I had a realisation that I didn't have to abandon my profession in totality, but that I could, in fact, make a contribution to its reinvention.

Then in 2014, I spent a year at *The School of Philosophy*, which along with the *Conscious Capitalism* movement inspired the thinking behind *Slow School*. The school was (and still is) my learn-by-doing experiment and a way to actually prove that I can build something powerful based on the philosophies in *Conscious Marketing*.

These past years have been an intense and restorative re-learning period. Even writing this book for you has been an incredible learning experience. It seems that the more I write, the more I learn!

PETER'S STORY

Peter Hutton is the principal of the public school, Templestowe College (TC). In his TEDx talk he opens with, "I hated school".

When he first started primary school, Peter had trouble with reading and spelling. "I knew I was smart. I just couldn't do some of the things others did, so I became the class clown and pretty much cheated and hustled my way through", says Peter. In high school, now at an elite private school, everything turned even worse. The culture of the school was violent, constrictive and testosterone fuelled. If asked to read out loud in class, he would either refuse outright or create a distraction that would result in him being punished. Being hit with a stick was preferable to the humiliation of reading in front of his peers. (At age 27, Peter was diagnosed with dyslexia and he finally understood why he hated school so much.)

Despite this, he was a smart young man with an eye for numbers and business, so he started a business building home units when he left school. At the time, in the early '80s he was making exorbitant amounts of money and living the high-life. And then, life took a big u-turn. The recession hit and he lost everything he owned (and almost his parent's home which had been mortgaged to fund the business).

At this point Peter came very close to taking his own life but instead took off to Cape Tribulation for a while to contemplate his next stage in life.

"When you define yourself by how much money you have then lose it all, your self-worth goes down the rabbit hole. Money is a very shaky foundation on which to build your life," reflects Peter.

Many years later in 2010, Peter came to TC. The school had an uncertain future as student enrolment had dropped from 1000 to 286 over a ten-year period. "There was a loyal band of hardworking teachers, parents and students when I got there," says Peter. "We had one year to turn it around. I pitched to the school board a new mission [purpose] 'to help students take control of their own learning' and the rest is history."

TC is now leading the way in education, with all eyes on the revolutionary model they've adopted. "The education system operates under an outdated, industrial model," says Peter. "It's lost its purpose and has no power to transform kids' lives. The qualities they're teaching: obedience, conformity and rote-learning are not skills needed for their future."

According to Dr Michael Carr-Gregg, a psychologist specialising in parenting and adolescence, 30% of youth in year 12 in Australia have diagnosable depression and 40% have an anxiety order. "How unfair is it, that at the very time youth are going through the turbulence of adolescence and puberty, that we put them into a system that defines them by testing and numbers," declares Peter. "The shift required is a philosophical one. We can't afford to hold a fixed mind-set on any issue regarding education. We need to let go of the control and command model and let kids take charge of their own learning. We must stop 'doing education' to kids and give them a choice in what they learn," says Peter.

At TC, there's no standard hours of attendance, no bells, no year levels and no hierarchies. Everyone is expected to perform to a high standard while students and teachers receive equal respect. Students choose what they most want to learn according to their passions and interests and are supported to start their own enterprise if that's their desire.

TC has now rebuilt to 1000 students with extensive waiting lists. The 'take control' approach to education is also gaining global attention and Peter is now bringing the model to other schools. In just eight months, Mount Alexander school (a school with a large number of non-English-speaking students) adopted the TC model with outstanding results. Peter's goal is now to take their approach to as many schools that are ready, willing and able.

 Watch Peter Hutton's TEDx talk on The Slow School of Business YouTube channel.

TIME TO PRACTISE

Meditation & Reflection	Find a quiet spot where you'll be uninterrupted or go for a silent walk to reflect on the following questions. Do this exercise for at least 30 minutes while breathing fully into it. Try to drop into your body and your heart as much as possible and feel the answers and not over-think it.
	Trace back through your life starting from your earliest memory. What were the main lessons you learnt and accepted without question from important and influential people and institutions in your life (parents, school, teachers, partners, church)? It can be helpful to do it in the following format: from my mother, I learnt... from my father, I learnt...from my school, I learnt... from my grade-five teacher, I learnt... from the church, I learnt...from the media, I learnt... from my first job, I learnt...from my partner, I learnt...and so on.
	Keep doing this until you can think of all the lessons you've learnt along the way. Don't judge the lessons, they are neither good nor bad, they just are.
	From all of these lessons, which are the lessons you wish to keep? Which are the lessons that you no longer need and wish to eliminate? What are the new things you have a desire to learn about now that might be directed towards your calling? Where and how will you learn about them? How might you create your own free-range re-learning program? What might that look like to you? How will re-learning help you to reach your highest potential?

Journaling Exercise	Now write for 30 minutes on the following: 1. Journal about all the answers to the questions in your meditation and reflection exercise. 2. How satisfied are you with your current re-learning regime? (Rank 1-10: 1 being really dissatisfied, 10 being very satisfied) 3. How satisfied would you like to be with your re-learning regime? (Rank 1-10 as above) 4. What is the gap? Identify how large the gap is between questions 2 and 3 to determine how much of a priority this practice is. 5. Set an intention for this practice. "I will practise re-learning by..." "I will know when I have fulfilled this intention when..."
Daily Practice	Identify at least one firm daily practice you'll adopt to change what you learn and how you learn it. What is it? How will you ensure you undertake this daily practice?
Big Action	Identify one big re-learning practice/activity you will undertake this week. What is it? When and how will you do it?

PRACTICE 5
THE PRACTICE OF BECOMING CONSCIOUS

> *Keep your thoughts positive, because your thoughts become your words.*
>
> *Keep your words positive, because your words become your behaviour.*
>
> *Keep your behaviour positive, because your behaviour becomes your habits.*
>
> *Keep your habits positive, because your habits become your values.*
>
> *Keep your values positive, because your values become your destiny.*
>
> - Mahatma Gandhi

Imagine an iceberg floating in the Antarctic. Two-thirds of the iceberg is floating beneath the water with only one-third of it visible above the water. The larger chunk below the water has the power to shift the whole iceberg in whichever direction it chooses. Now imagine that iceberg is your mind. The part below the water is your unconscious mind and the part above the water is your conscious mind. Just like the iceberg, your unconscious mind has the power to direct your conscious mind and, therefore, direct your life.

Freud defined the unconscious mind as a reservoir of feelings, thoughts, urges and memories that are outside our awareness. He believed that most of the contents of our unconscious mind are unacceptable or unpleasant, such as feelings of pain, anxiety or conflict and that they influence our behaviour even though we're unaware of them. Your unconscious mind can sway you towards pessimism or optimism, negative thinking or positive thinking, sadness or happiness.

Victimhood is a very powerful unconscious belief of many humans. We blame others for our work or life situation. We're the victim of our partner, our parents, our boss, our government. Most notably, however, we're the victims of our own limited thinking. Stepping out of our unconscious victimhood is essential to become a practitioner of purpose.

This means clearing away the deeply in-grained faulty thinking and behaviour. You shine a light on those old negative patterns of thinking that have kept you stuck. You throw out those comfortable but dirty and worn-out old thoughts. You do the deep work and get excruciatingly honest with yourself.

You work diligently with your counsellor, a psychologist or a therapist. You revisit the events in your life that were both painful and joyful. You acknowledge and examine the thoughts that arise. You journal about them but you don't judge them. You consciously keep them if they're positive and helpful - and give them away if they're not. You take up daily practices that bring your consciousness to the fore, practices like yoga, journaling, meditation, prayer and walking barefoot on the grass.

You practise being in the now, not the past, not the future, but the right here and now – in the present, by slowing down and connecting to all the senses. You wipe the dishes slowly and study the pattern on the plate. You examine each leaf and flower as you garden. You cook methodically and lovingly. You go to the playground with your children and leave your phone at home to play make-believe with them. You smell the pungent, earthy smell of cows in the field. You inhale deeply and exhale fully and notice the rise and fall of your belly. As much as you possibly can, you enter a child-like state of wonder and curiosity.

When it comes to your work, you are present to each task that you complete. You consider these questions. What am I enjoying about this task? What am I not enjoying? What am I learning? Is the outcome something I'm proud of? Did I savour the experience, or did I rush through it? Is this a task I would rather not do? Is there something else I would rather do? You recognise when you're in flow or when you're bored or anxious. You recognise your strengths and weaknesses, your likes and dislikes and those things that put a spring in your step or that kill your enthusiasm.

Henry Ford said, "whether you think you can or think you can't, you're right". Taking steps towards fulfilling your life's work, requires you to first believe that it's entirely possible. You become aware when your monkey mind starts chattering with thoughts of impossibility. You stop and remind yourself that you are not your mind, that your thoughts are just conditioned reactions to your past and projections about your future. You constantly refocus your thoughts on the positive and direct them towards your calling. And then you don't just think about it, you turn your positive thoughts into powerful deeds.

If our negative, unconscious thinking and conditioning remains more powerful than our commitment to fulfil our reason for being, we'll remain forever ineffective and incapable of realising our dream. We must do all we can, therefore, to continue our practice of becoming conscious.

Many years ago, Billy and I were on a road-trip with my Dad and stepmother. We were visiting all the small country towns we'd lived in when I was growing up. As we were driving through the countryside and as Billy was fast asleep, I pulled out *The Power of Now* by Eckhart Tolle. The book is a guide for day-to-day living and stresses the importance of living in the present moment. Tolle teaches that our mode of consciousness can be transformed and that the key to becoming free of the ego and its unhappy consequences, is to become deeply conscious of the now.

I was just three pages into the book when I received a bolt of lightning to the brain. I just knew that my life was being driven by the sadness of the past and anxiety about the future. I stared out the window and tears of relief took over. It felt like a blessing that I'd finally diagnosed my dis-ease - a lack of capacity to live in the present. And the irony didn't escape me that I was on a road-trip digging up my past while discovering the power of the present!

That book was the catalyst for me to start pursuing a spiritual path and a deeper level of consciousness. It opened the door to reading and learning more, to practising meditation, yoga and journaling and so much more.

Taking steps towards fulfilling your life's work, requires you to first believe that it's entirely possible.

Like all perfectly imperfect human beings, at times, I do allow my unconscious conditioned patterns of the past to creep in for a while (thankfully only very fleetingly these days). I've worked hard to shine a light on my old negative thinking and behaviours: saying yes to everyone to please them and avoid conflict; wanting everyone to like me and the fear of rejection; and undervaluing myself and my skills, experience and talents.

As a middle-aged white woman who has grown up in the rather conservative culture that exists in Australia, I've also had to strongly reject the societal conditioning that has greatly contributed to this thinking and behaviour. For these patterns are not mine alone. I believe they're the dominant limiting thoughts and behaviours of many women and it's why we've not made the progress we need to bring about true equality.

More than ever today, we need women everywhere to get over their negative unconscious conditioning, to clear their faulty thinking, to stop conceding and start leading from their powerful feminine essence in partnership with our powerful masculine counterparts.

BETH'S STORY

One morning in May 2015, Beth Jennings woke up and realised things had to change. "I'd studied photography at one of the best universities in the world and been a photographer for 20 years. I looked at my bank account and discovered I couldn't pay my credit card bill. I had this gut-wrenching feeling of failure," shares Beth. "When I graduated, I was dead sure I'd do well in photography because I'd been to this amazing institute and my standard was high. The realisation that I hadn't achieved my dream, turned my shame into fear. I felt that my life shouldn't be like this and I was scared about the future." This was the catalyst for Beth to start the journey to put her limiting beliefs under the microscope. She spent six weeks in solitude. "It was a total 'pens-down' period and I did no work. I sat on the couch for hours, rested a lot and didn't speak to anyone. My life to that point had felt like a moving roller-coaster that I couldn't get off. Here I was now, finally getting off," reflects Beth.

Beth traced back through her life journey and thought deeply about her prevailing mind-set. "I'd been a wedding photographer for four years, had a break for two years, then travelled and photographed in four different continents in nine years," says Beth. "I'd done exactly what I'd wanted work-wise, but I was consistently financially challenged. It was an unhealthy recurring pattern."

While Beth believed in the quality of her photography, she lacked the confidence to promote her services and think beyond the basics of the commercial nature of it. "I'd always ask myself questions like: what's next; what products can I offer; how am I going to do that; who would even want that? These questions were constrictive rather than expansive and I had no concept of my potential."

During the six weeks Beth started asking herself some different questions. 'What does Beth want to offer the world? What would make Beth happy? What is the photography the world needs to see from Beth?'

She got curious and creative, opened her heart and dropped into the passion she felt for her craft. She explored its true potential to both make an impact on people and create prosperity. One idea was to photograph the real personalities of business people rather than what the world expects to see such as the standard headshot.

"I rang my friend Christian who's an equine soft tissue therapist. I asked if he'd help me explore a new way of photography I was testing. He said yes straight away. The result had a big impact on Christian and it was affirmation that I'd found my *why*. It helped me value my work in a whole new way."

Nearly two years later, Beth consciously chooses who she puts in front of her camera. "I'm drawn to photographing business leaders who are here to assist humanity and who want to share what really matters in the world. I'm now in the driver's seat and I have way less fear. I just keep doing the work, getting better at it and asking for the fee I'm worth."

Beth has also changed so many other things about her way of life. "I eat well. I follow a mostly Paleo diet. I get good sleep. I meditate each morning, follow it with a walk and do yoga. I journal daily and list the things I'm grateful for. I'm conscious about the friendships I nurture and the clients I take on. That break-down period was a break-through for me. It wasn't fun, but I'm super glad now that it happened," ends Beth.

Watch Beth Jennings talk on The Slow School of Business YouTube channel.

TIME TO PRACTISE

Meditation & Reflection	Find a quiet spot where you'll be uninterrupted or go for a silent walk to reflect on the following questions. Do this exercise for at least 30 minutes while breathing fully into it. Try to drop into your body and your heart as much as possible and feel the answers and not over-think it.

Reread Karen's story on page 70. Imagine you're about to have a meeting with your manager. If you work for yourself, imagine yourself as the boss. Assume you're currently working in your profession (the intersection of 'what you are good at' and 'what you can be paid for') but you're not being fulfilled or doing what you love.

You've reconnected with that thing you're truly passionate about (name it, no matter how wild!) and you want to bring it into your current work and get a pay rise! You want to pitch a *Purpose Project* to your boss.

Firstly, think about the negative self-talk that might prevent you from asking for what you want. Say the statements out loud and feel them deep in your heart. Now take three deep breaths and consciously say the opposite of those statements out loud.

Now play out the same scenario under your positive, 'anything is possible' thinking. Imagine yourself stating your desire and asking for what you want. How does it feel? What are you saying? What is the response? What will you do now with this exercise? What is the first step? When will you take it?

How will becoming more conscious each day help you to reach your highest potential? What does an ever-increasing conscious life look like for you? Imagine a day in that life.

Journaling Exercise	Now write for 30 minutes on the following:

1. Journal about all the answers to the questions in your meditation and reflection exercise.

2. How satisfied are you with your current level of consciousness?
   (Rank 1-10: 1 being really dissatisfied, 10 being very satisfied)

3. How satisfied would you like it to be?
   (Rank 1-10 as above)

4. What is the gap? Identify how large the gap is between questions 2 and 3 to determine how much of a priority this practice is.

5. Set an intention for this practice.
   "I will practise becoming more conscious by..."
   "I will know when I have fulfilled this intention when..."

Daily Practice	Identify at least one firm daily practice you'll adopt to become more conscious. What is it? How will you ensure you undertake this daily practice?
Big Action	Identify one big action you will undertake this week to become more conscious. What is it? When and how will you do it?

PRACTICE 6
THE PRACTICE OF REDEFINING SUCCESS

*Don't aim for success if you want it; just do what
you love and believe in, and it will come naturally.*
- David Frost

'The Golden Handcuffs' was a phrase first coined in the 1970s in reference to the financial compensation employees would receive for staying with a company. Today these handcuffs include stock options, bonuses, paid long service leave and a whole host of other financial incentives. Take a moment to imagine those golden handcuffs on your wrists. Quite a provocative image, isn't it?

Today we can broaden out that metaphor and apply it to many areas of life. The golden handcuffs may come in the form of multiple homes with insurmountable debt, years of private school fees and expensive lifestyles.

Western society has a toxic, unhealthy definition of success. How wealthy you are, how many qualifications you have, your job title, where you live and where you went to school, are our limited measures of success and, therefore, our worth.

We must rewrite the book of success if we're going to lead a purposeful and prosperous life. We must shift the success narrative away from what we possess to what really matters: how healthy we are, how lightly we live on our planet, how we treat others, how we contribute to community and whether we're pursuing work that's meaningful.

> We must rewrite the book of success if we're going to lead a purposeful and prosperous life. We must shift the success narrative away from what we possess to what really matters.

> Purpose is a stable and generalized intention to accomplish something that is at the same time meaningful to the self and consequential for the world beyond the self.
>
> - William Damon

The practice of redefining what success means for you, requires real courage. It requires you to honestly scrutinise those things in your life that are your golden handcuffs and to find the key to unlocking and releasing them.

This doesn't mean giving everything away and living in a tent in the middle of nowhere. It means slowly redefining success through shedding any burdensome layers of materiality you might have so that you can return to your essence. It means removing The Golden Handcuffs and returning to your Golden Buddha.

So how do you do this?

You start at your death. You imagine a celebration of your life at your funeral. You're surrounded by family and friends. They're sharing stories of your life that reveal the depth of your soul and the length of your legacy. Then you return from the dead and you consider the life you're living now. If you died tomorrow, what stories would your loved ones be sharing?

You let the incongruence of this scenario sink right in. Then you surrender to it. You don't condemn it or judge it, for you are not broken. You make a commitment to put your old definition of success (and your current lifestyle, work or business) under the microscope, and you slowly shift towards a new way of being. You return to those things you stand for and believe in and you become intensely aware of where things are out of alignment.

Then you revisit the definition of purpose and make it your own definition for success.

Purpose is a stable and generalized intention to accomplish something that is at the same time meaningful to the self and consequential for the world beyond the self. -William Damon

Remember the three elements of this definition: a stable and generalised intention to accomplish something (a *Purpose Project*), that is meaningful to the self (that really matters to you) and consequential to the world beyond the self (that is in service to others).

You become a practitioner of this new version of success. You gently and slowly analyse your health, your belongings, your finances, your work or business, your relationships, your friends, your home, your day-to-day life-style. You start with that thing that's the biggest challenge for you right now. You make small daily shifts and sometimes even titanic shifts.

Success is not a thing to acquire, it's a daily practice. It's a way of being and behaving in every moment of every day. It's a feeling you have. It's the feeling of joy you have in your daily accomplishments as they're deeply aligned with your values and beliefs. It's about living by your personal manifesto - a public declaration of your intentions, beliefs and aspirations.

It's time. Time to change your definition of success and place your success ladder up a new wall so you can become everything you were born to be, and then some!

I've personally struggled a lot with how to measure the success of *Slow School*. The business world has a very narrow definition of success, and it's based on quantitative measures such as revenue, profit and market share. A business can be viewed as wildly successful if it meets its financial targets, even as it extracts maximum value from all its stakeholders and leaves them depleted. This is not my definition of success!

When I first started the school in 2014, I didn't have a business model or a proven formula for how I would make revenue. There was no way I was going to follow the tired old funnel marketing approach (the '7-steps from rags to riches' programs) that so many business people were peddling either. I wanted to do it my way by treating *Slow School* as more of a community and a movement rather than a business.

Six months in, we'd had 500 people to classes, dinners and events. We had oodles of purpose, lots of market presence and a wonderful community of purpose-driven entrepreneurs contributing voluntarily to the cause. And personally, I was having the time of my life!

While I didn't have to invest any money in the school, we weren't making much money and we didn't have a clear service offering, so I had to come up with a solution pronto. I was out walking one evening and came up with the idea for *Talk on Purpose* (called 'Is there a TED talk in you?' at the time). I wondered how I might engage the *Slow School* community to create a course that would bring purpose to the workplace, while making us all prosperous.

It's been a labour of love, but now we've prototyped and tested the product with over 80 graduates and we're pitching it to schools and companies. We know with certainty that this course changes people's lives. We've been there to see it, to feel it and sit with our course participants as they breathe their way through their fear and discomfort so they can shift their work-life to a whole new level. These are all people who are now having a 'purpose ripple effect' amongst their families, co-workers, clients and their community.

That, in my terms, is the ultimate definition of success. Although we still have a long way to go to achieve success in terms of solid and consistent prosperity, we can now see a clear pathway forward.

When you're doing what you truly love, and being of service to others, success will come. It just requires a fresh perspective on what success actually is and patience and persistence as you bring your *Purpose Project* to life.

PENNY'S STORY

I first met Penny Locaso at Kinfolk Café in Melbourne for a coffee in early 2015. Penny had reached out to me for some inspiration on what to do next in her career. She was at the end of a six-month sabbatical from work and had recently moved from Perth to Melbourne with her four-year-old son and separated from her husband. I was struck by how similar her story was to my own and how open and willing she was to explore all the possibilities that might lead her to a new livelihood.

"I worked in a senior role at Shell for over 15 years and then last year as we were restructuring, I was offered a redundancy package," says Penny. "At the same time, I was being headhunted by BHP, so I was potentially looking at a pay-out and a new job which would have been a financial boon for me. As it turned out, I didn't end up getting the BHP job. It was actually quite a profound 'sliding doors' moment."

The experience made Penny realise she wanted something different for the next stage of her working life, so she gave herself permission to take six months off. She stopped applying for corporate jobs and had as many coffees as she could with passionate, purpose-driven business people. She gave herself the grace to explore and experiment with various ideas and to build her networks.

Penny is brutally honest about the very narrow perspective she had on what success actually was for her. Through her working life, she'd bought into the notion that success was measured by how quickly she'd climbed the ranks, the car she drove, the home she had and the brands she wore. "In the process, I lost that connection to who I was as a woman. I'd taken on all these roles as a worker, a mother, a wife and I didn't have much idea of what I loved or was passionate about beyond my son."

Within six months of our coffee, Penny launched her own business, BKindred and she's been on a fast-paced learn-by-doing journey ever since. What she started just 12 months ago already looks vastly different as Penny constantly revisits the ikigai purpose model and drills down on her purpose.

Through practice she's gained clarity on her purpose, which she now shares far and wide with others. "My purpose is to empower women to lead happier lives by building courage, clarity, connection and the tactical skills to make change," states Penny firmly and clearly. "I am working on my purpose every day now. I set goals for the year and I plan my work as a series of 90-day projects. I'm fundamentally okay with not knowing what's around the corner and with not being wedded to a long-term plan," says Penny.

Penny now defines success by three simple things: the impact she has on the lives of others, the happiness she feels inside and her level of presence as a parent. "I've radically reframed what success means to me and I've never been more fulfilled in my adult life. My advice to anyone wanting to redefine success and make change happen, is to create the headspace to think about this stuff and work out what you really want. Success requires the whitespace to dream and create."

 Watch Penny Locaso's talk on The Slow School of Business YouTube channel.

TIME TO PRACTISE

Meditation & Reflection	Find a quiet spot where you'll be uninterrupted or go for a silent walk to reflect on the following questions. Do this exercise for at least 30 minutes while breathing fully into it.
	Try to drop into your body and your heart as much as possible and feel the answers and not over-think it. (Warning: You may need tissues for this practice.)
	You're at your own funeral looking down on the crowd gathered. Where is it? Who is there? What kind of day is it? Imagine all the people that you love one by one stepping forward for your eulogy and sharing a story about you and saying what they love about you.
	Breathe in deeply as you envision each person, place them right in your heart. As they share something about you, they're looking directly into your eyes and hugging you tight.
	When you've finished this exercise, take three deep breaths and reflect on these questions. What were the consistent themes of your eulogy? What was the common measure of your success as a human being?
	What are you working on right now that is working towards this success? What is preventing you right now from working towards this success?
	What is your new definition of success now? What do you need to review and eliminate to achieve success? How will focusing on this new definition help you reach your highest potential?

Journaling Exercise	Now write for 30 minutes on the following:

1. Journal about all the answers to the questions in your meditation and reflection exercise.

2. How satisfied am I with my current level of success according to my new definition?
   (Rank 1-10: 1 being totally dissatisfied, 10 totally satisfied)

3. How satisfying would it be to live every day according to this new version of success?
   (Rank 1-10 as above)

4. What is the gap? Identify how large the gap is between questions 2 and 3. This will determine how much of a priority this practice is.

5. Set an intention for this practice.
   "I will practise reframing my view of success by…"
   "I will know when I have fulfilled this intention when…"

Daily Practice	Identify at least one firm daily practice you'll adopt to work towards your new definition of success. What is it? How will you ensure you undertake this daily practice?
Big Action	Identify one big action you will take in the next week to shift your overall success factor up a whole notch. What is it? When will you do it?

PRACTICE 7
THE PRACTICE OF CURIOSITY

Satisfaction of one's curiosity is one of the greatest sources of happiness in life.
- Linus Pauling

Like creativity, our education system all but killed off our innate sense of curiosity. If we showed a sense of curiosity outside the bounds of the curriculum, we were actively discouraged or even severely punished.

So, along the way, many of us never developed our curiosity gene. We never cultivated curiosity as a personality trait or habit. Without even realising it, we started to settle. We settled on our partner, our home, our city, our profession, our friends, our hobbies and our future. We settled on the music we liked, the genre of books we read, the movies we watched, the food we preferred and the places we liked to holiday. We swapped curiosity for certainty and thereby having to deal with the unexpected or the unfamiliar. We got stuck in our comfort zone and torpor took over.

As Henry Thoreau said, "most people live lives of quiet desperation and go to the grave with the music still in them". A healthy sense of curiosity will ensure this never happens!

If our capacity for curiosity is non-existent, it's nigh on impossible to fulfil our deepest potential. Curiosity didn't kill the cat, or humans for that matter. It's incuriosity that kills us and it's not an instant painless death. It's a long, slow, painful death from living an unfulfilled, boring life.

> Many of us never developed our curiosity gene. We never cultivated curiosity as a personality trait or habit. Without even realising it, we started to settle.

Finding this a bit strong? You can probably tell it's a practice I'm particularly passionate about. Our lack of curiosity is why so many people are dying at work. When we lose our curiosity to try something new or do something a different way, we die a little more every day. Awakening our capacity for curiosity is a most vital practice for bringing meaning to our work.

On the other hand, some of us developed an acute sense of curiosity to the point of suffering MPD (Multiple Possibility Disorder) and BSOD (Bright Shiny Object Disorder). These are both disorders that see us constantly distracted and trying new things yet never settling and showing commitment to a path. Our curiosity places us adrift on an ocean of possibility without the wherewithal to take a deep dive to the ocean floor and narrowly focus our attention.

So, it seems, the world is filled with both the incurious and the overly-curious with neither having just enough focused curiosity to gain crystal clear clarity on a way forward. At some point, we must take a stand and feed our curiosity by going deep and narrow. Curiosity becomes awareness. Awareness becomes attention. Attention becomes interest. Interest becomes desire. Desire becomes intention. Intention becomes action. We pick a *Purpose Project*. We test and experiment. We rinse and repeat.

The people I most admire in the world are the risk-takers, the change-makers and the rebels. They're the ones constantly moving to the heartbeat of their curious lives, the ones that stop watching and start doing. They're the self-appointed leaders in organisations, in communities, in business. They haven't waited for a title, a job description or a pay-rise to explore the possibilities and be curious. They are just innately curious. They work in big companies and small. They're entrepreneurs. They're students. They're deeply curious about how to build a better world and they create movements of change through their work.

Intuition is the great partner of curiosity. Intuition guides you in determining what to investigate further. You follow a hunch to make contact with the author of a

On the other hand, some of us developed an acute sense of curiosity to the point of suffering MPD (Multiple Possibility Disorder) and BSOD (Bright Shiny Object Disorder).

book you loved that's in the field of your deepest interest. You see a post on social media about a course on a subject you've always secretly wanted to master, and you instantly book it. You meet someone at an event who is working in a field you're curious about, so you ask for their card and follow them up for a coffee. You volunteer for a cause you truly believe in, open to the idea that it might turn into your vocation. You try a new hobby and take that class you've always been curious about.

You replace the habits that have kept you incurious by doing one thing different every day. You take a new path each morning on your walk to work. You go to a local community event on the weekend that you might normally have avoided. You say 'yes' when in the past you would have said 'no'. You develop a keen interest in other people's ideas and opinions and you ask brilliant questions and listen for the answers. And in the process, you become both interested and interesting as a wholehearted human being.

You have everything you need to satisfy your curiosity when you have the world-wide-web at your fingertips and the whole-wide-world on your doorstep!

The end of 2015 and early 2016 was really challenging for me. I became an empty-nester with Billy leaving home and moving to college (a most painful experience for many parents). I'd exhausted myself with the running of two businesses and not seeing the financial return I'd anticipated and I was feeling unhealthy and lethargic. Many times, I sat alone at home feeling stuck and not knowing where to turn for help.

My 'stuck-ness' had killed my curiosity and, therefore, my capacity for expansion. While I wasn't depressed, I most definitely felt debilitated. The one thing that kept me stable and moving forward, was my writing. There was not a day that I did not write – whether that was journaling, writing blogs or this book. The very thing that gave me most meaning, was bigger than the difficult circumstances I was dealing with.

I guess it's not the image you would have of a woman who's living and working at the intersection of her purpose! It's a reminder, though, that I'm human and that we all get stuck, even if we are 'on purpose'. It's also a reminder that I must practise what I preach!

Over the course of a few months, I just fully surrendered to my situation. I found the courage to share the truth with a counsellor who then encouraged me to share the truth with my father. After 15 years of being fiercely independent as a lone-mother-wolf and independent businesswoman, I asked my Dad for help. It was terrifying and humiliating yet incredibly freeing.

I felt empowered to make some bold and uncomfortable changes to free myself from my 'stuck-ness' which included selling my home, appointing a new business coach and taking a new approach to each of my businesses. These changes enabled me to once more cultivate and expand my curiosity and creativity and they took me one giant step closer towards fulfilling my reason for being.

Pain always leads you deeper into your purpose. It's there to test your resolve and your resilience and your commitment to doing the work you're meant to be doing.

JULIE AND MARC'S STORY

Julie Bennett has been one of my dearest and closest friends since 2001. I met her at one of the first networking events I held in Sydney when I started my first business. I loved Julie from the moment I met her. She was (and still is) vivacious, generous, creative and very, very curious about life and all its possibilities.

Over all these years, our friendship has led us to working together, living together, travelling together, crying together and laughing together. We've shared our pains, our joys and everything in between. Julie has always been a brave woman who I admire and respect.

"About seven years ago, at age 41, I was forced to close my business due to financial hardship. I lost my home, my car, my savings and my business and I only had a handful of possessions left," reminisces Julie. "It was an incredibly humiliating and humbling experience. It required my full surrender and there were many times I just wasn't sure how I would get through it. Somehow I found the courage to get up every day and keep moving forward instead of just collapsing and giving up."

Not surprisingly, Julie was keen for a new start in a new country outside Australia. She'd been to Boulder, Colorado in the USA a few months earlier and decided that was where she wanted to live. She found a company to employ and sponsor her, sold her remaining possessions and then flew back to Boulder to start her new job. While her pay was meagre, and she was barely making ends meet, Julie finally started to feel hopeful again that her life was heading in a new direction.

"While I'd been going through these huge changes, I'd been shut off to the potential of finding a life partner. Once I'd settled in Boulder and recovered from the trauma of my financial situation, I started putting myself out there and dating again. Then one day it just happened. I met the love of my life, Marc. One year later we were married and we settled into domestic bliss in a modest home with 9 to 5 jobs," says Julie.

Two years later, Julie and Marc were sharing their dreams for their life with each other. The conversation turned into curiosity about what life could be like outside the confines of conventional living. Their curiosity led to a year of intense investigations into how they could make a living on the road while exploring the wonders of the USA.

In 2014, they sold their home and everything in it, bought an RV (travelling motorhome) and transitioned their careers to support remote working from the road. Now three years later, they've travelled across 49 of the 50 USA states all while sharing their journey on their very popular blog and *RVLoveTV* YouTube channel which has now had over a million views. Their current project is now all about inspiring others considering living the RV lifestyle through the *RV Success School* which helps educate and guide people to make sound decisions, avoid expensive mistakes and ensure their success on the road.

Taking the leap truly changed both of their lives and their careers.

"I had no idea when I first went to the US, that my work-life purpose would become all about bringing the same freedom that Marc and I experience, to thousands of others. We know our *why* and that's what keeps us committed and focused on our work. Our willingness to be curious, experiment and explore was the key to finding our path. We also have incredible fun together and don't take things too seriously," ends Julie.

Visit RVLoveTV and The Slow School of Business YouTube channel.

TIME TO PRACTISE

Meditation & Reflection	Before starting this exercise, read some of the highlights of your journal from the ikigai purpose questions. Find a quiet spot where you'll be uninterrupted or go for a silent walk to reflect on the following scenarios.

Do this exercise for at least 30 minutes while breathing fully into it. Try to drop into your body and your heart as much as possible and feel the answers and not over-think it. Reflect on any/all of the following scenarios.

Scenario 1:

Imagine all the jobs/businesses you could possibly be curious about exploring further. Choose one that you could be insatiably curious about and go deep. What is the job? What would you be doing day-to-day in that job/business? Where is it? Who are you with? What are some steps you could take right now to explore it?

Scenario 2:

Imagine yourself at your current job/business. How satisfied with it are you right now? (Score 1-10: 1 being totally dissatisfied and 10 being totally satisfied).

What would make it more satisfying? What ideas could you get curious about and explore to bring more purpose to your daily work? How could you bring a greater sense of curiosity to your co-workers/team?

Scenario 3:

What areas outside of work (hobbies/interests) are you curious to explore?

What might a curious week look like for you?

What would you be doing? Who would you be with? Where would you be?

How will a greater sense of curiosity help you reach your highest potential?

Journaling Exercise	Now write for 30 minutes on the following:

1. Journal about all the answers to the questions in your meditation and reflection exercise.

2. What is your current curiosity factor when it comes to your work/life?
   (Rank 1-10: 1 being totally incurious, 10 being totally curious)

3. What would you like your curiosity factor to be?
   (Rank 1-10 as above)

4. What is the gap? Identify how large the gap is between questions 2 and 3 to determine how much of a priority this practice is.

5. Set an intention for this practice.
   "I will practise more curiosity by..."
   "I will know when I have fulfilled this intention when..."

Daily Practice	From the meditation and journaling exercise, identify at least one firm daily practice you will adopt to bring more curiosity to your life and work.
Big Action	Identify one big action you will take in the next week to shift your overall curiosity factor up a whole notch. What is it? When will you do it?

PRACTICE 8
THE PRACTICE OF CREATIVITY

" Creativity is always a leap of faith. You're faced with a blank page, blank easel, or an empty stage. "
- Julia Cameron

At some point in our life, just like we did with curiosity and courage, many of us unwittingly gave up on the exploration and cultivation of our innate creativity. The clay of our life circumstances hid our creative genius.

That clay often appeared as the opinion of others which resulted in our self-limiting beliefs. We had a teacher tell us we'd never become a singer that day we sang one note off-key. We had parents diligently directing us away from acting towards a more 'sensible career'. We put down that paintbrush the day the careers advisor told us we had a talent for numbers and a future in accounting.

We told ourselves that we didn't have the real talent for our art. We accepted the judgement of others as the truth and we never questioned the false assumption that our creativity could never lead us to our livelihood. That was the day we sold ourselves short and our creative soul died. It was the day we chose the rational route to work.

Creativity [noun]: the use of the imagination or original ideas, especially in the production of an artistic work.

This definition has three very important components: use of imagination; original ideas; and the production of an artistic work.

"The man who has no imagination, has no wings," said Muhammad Ali. Imagination is the starting point for creating our reality. First we must conceive it, if we are to create it. We must imagine ourselves being that thing we really wish to become. We must imagine ourselves doing that thing we really wish to do.

"The merit of originality is not novelty; it is sincerity," said Thomas Carlisle. So many of us believe we're not creative because we fear we're not 'original', that we'll be seen as an imitation, a poor copy of others. However, 'original' does not mean our work has never been conceived of before. It means going back to our source, the place where something begins, our origins. Originality is actually the culmination of our life experiences and learning and it's rooted in sincerity. From originality, we're free to create, despite what others have done before us.

It's from imagination and originality, that you create your work of art. You paint your masterpiece. You perform in a play. You write a blog. You photograph your street. And then you extend that work of art into a greater artistic project. You write a play and bring it to life at your kid's school. You write and publish your first book. You photograph your whole neighbourhood and hold an exhibition in a local gallery. Then you expand your creative repertoire to include singing, designing and dancing.

And you don't need to be an art-maker to be creative. You are creative in your cooking, gardening and homemaking. You are creative when you tell your children made-up bedtime stories. You are creative when you sing and dance at home with your family. You are creative in the way you live. Creativity is life, and in so doing, life expands beyond limits. You're not just a creative voyeur. You're a creative doer. You're a practitioner of creativity.

You may, or may not, choose to make a living from your creative talents. You may instead, bring the creative talents you've cultivated outside of work, right into work. You bring your drawing, singing, music, poetry, writing and design talents, to your desk. You make them as revered and applauded as your capacity to produce a spreadsheet, process a customer order or write a business report. You share your art with your co-workers and your customers. In so doing you bring love and healing to the workplace.

> Imagination is the starting point for creating our reality. First we must conceive it, if we are to create it.

Creativity is the foundation of innovation. Creativity is what births an idea, while innovation is what brings it to life. Creativity is about imagination, while innovation is about execution. Creativity comes from the heart. Innovation comes from the head. Innovation without creativity is nothing.

Creativity is not simply the domain of the marketing department used as the backbone of clever advertising campaigns. Creativity is the underlying principle adopted by every person, in every department, every day. Creativity is the backbone of leadership, problem solving, teamwork, project management and employee engagement. Creativity is the backbone of a healthy, vibrant, loving culture. In fact, creativity *is* culture.

Courage leads to curiosity. Curiosity leads to creativity. Creativity comes from surrendering. Creativity expands when we are in nature. Creativity is rooted in child-like wonder. Creativity leads to a fulfilling life and meaningful work.

One of my most productive creative spurts was in Aix-en-Provence, France. I arrived in Aix with a blank page ready to write *Real Women,* a book of stories of women who'd overcome adversity. I'd chosen the women, outlined the chapters of the book and set my writing goals. However, each time I sat down to write, my creativity would desert me. I'd get a severe case of writer's block. Then instead of busting through it, I'd find myself busting out and exploring.

I'd find myself immersed in the culture of the town. I'd stroll through the galleries, meditate in the churches and ensconce myself in a corner of a café to listen to the sounds of the French conversing over lunch with the bustle of the farmers' markets close by. I'd write pages and pages in my journal. I'd do yoga, do lunch, do coffee. I'd do anything but write. I was living creatively in the hope that I'd *become* creative.

Then one night, I went to bed and posed the question to myself. "Should I be writing *Real Women*, or should I be writing about my own journey?" The next morning my journal answered, "write about your own journey and this time in France. Capture this experience while you're having it. It's essential for your healing and eventually it will help other women too". From that moment on, I chose to fill my blank page with what my heart was calling me to do. The words, sentences and paragraphs flowed. Some were good, some not so good, and I didn't care. It was not my job to judge the words. It was my job to make my art. It was my job to unleash my imagination and tap into my originality, my source.

My writing was also the catalyst for developing an interest in photography. I was compelled to capture my experience in both words and images. Each day I'd take my camera out to shoot the delights of Aix. I discovered for myself, albeit as a complete novice, how to work with the light, capture the essence of a scene and an expression on a face. I discovered the power of looking up, looking ahead and looking deeply into the nooks and crannies. Because of the camera, my experience of Aix was profoundly deepened. I noticed more, I felt more and it appeared in the power of my words on the pages of my book.

And finally, this creative experience has been etched indelibly in my memory so that it's now become the inspiration for the experience I wish to create in writing my next book!

ANNALIE'S STORY

Since the age of 19, when she first experienced New York City, Annalie Killian has had a dream to work there. Just one year ago, the 54-year-old, single-mother of two daughters made her dream a reality.

"With the children's high school years behind them, I no longer felt the pull of having to put their needs ahead of my own career aspirations," says Annalie. "I could have opted for a predictable and comfortable countdown to retirement in Sydney where I'd been the mastermind behind AMP's Amplify event for 10 years, or I could finally fulfil my dream and start a totally new career in the city that never sleeps; New York."

"You're not done just because you turn 50," says Annalie, "I just knew I was about to enter the most creative period of my life. I still had more to give to the world and I was under-utilised and bored in a role that wasn't going anywhere. I knew that if I didn't take the plunge, I'd regret it", she says.

Annalie quit her job, sold her house, packed up her life and moved to New York with three cats in tow. Within weeks, she was offered a role at the disruptor of Madison Avenue, sparks & honey - a trend-analysis and strategic foresight firm that combines the best of data science and human creativity to analyse change in real time to turn it into product innovation and new business models.

This wasn't Annalie's first international leap of faith. Before coming to Australia in 1999, she'd held leadership roles at BHP in Zululand, South Africa. The company was building the largest aluminium refinery in the world and it was a tense time in the lead-up to the transition from apartheid to democracy following the release of Nelson Mandela in 1991. Annalie was one of the first women to be appointed to a management position in an all-white male leadership team. There was not a single black person in leadership and her role was to introduce a program to upskill employees to address the problems they encountered on the job.

"I had to draw on every creative bone in my body to make my work relevant and ensure that everyone had an equal opportunity to participate, acquire skills and knowledge and that they were treated with dignity. I became an internal activist, a change agent from within and I was fortunate to be able to shape my role to meet the changing demands of a new South Africa. The experience was profound and it established my work purpose, for life," says Annalie.

While technology and innovation have been instrumental to each job in her life, Annalie's purpose has remained a steadfastly human one. "My purpose is to catalyse the magic of human beings to help them live their best and most self-actualised lives," she says with certainty. "Machines and technology are a medium for innovation but as leaders we need to always put humanity and the enablement of human potential first. It's about combining humanity with technology."

What's been most encouraging in learning about Annalie's career, is how she's stayed true to herself and her values without compromising herself. Instead of becoming a corporate escapee and starting her own business like so many do, she's brought a blank canvas to each of her roles and made that canvas her own. She's brought humanity and creativity to work and sets an excellent example that anything is possible. "If we can imagine it, we can create it," claims Annalie.

TIME TO PRACTISE

Meditation & Reflection	Find a quiet spot where you'll be uninterrupted or go for a silent walk to reflect on the following scenarios. Do this exercise for at least 30 minutes while breathing fully into it. Try to drop into your body and your heart as much as possible and feel the answers and not over-think it. Reflect on the happy creative moments that stand out from your life both at home and/or work. Start from your earliest memories as a child to where you are right now. Settle on one of the most profoundly creative moments. Sit in that moment for a minute. Bring it to the front of your memory in detail. Where were you? What were you doing or creating? Dancing, painting, singing? Who were you with? What was happening? How did you feel? What happened after that, where did that experience lead you? Let that experience go and think of another experience and go through the same questions. Feel into your creative potential. How might you bring that beautiful child-like creativity into your daily life? What might you do next with this untapped creativity? How could you bring it into your work? How will greater creativity help you to reach your highest potential?
Journaling Exercise	Now write for 30 minutes on the following: 1. Journal about all the answers to the questions in your meditation and reflection exercise. 2. What is your current creativity factor when it comes to your work? (Rank 1-10: 1 being totally uncreative, 10 being totally creative) 3. What would you like your creativity factor to be? (Rank 1-10 as above) 4. What is the gap? Identify how large the gap is between questions 2 and 3 to determine how much of a priority this practice is. 5. Set an intention for this practice. "I will practise more creativity by..." "I will know when I have fulfilled this intention when..."
Daily Practice	From the meditation and journaling exercise, identify at least one firm daily practice you will adopt to bring more creativity to your life and work.
Big Action	Identify one big action you will take in the next week to shift your overall creativity factor up a whole notch. What is it? When will you do it?

PRACTICE 9
THE PRACTICE OF LOVE & COMPASSION

" *Love and compassion are necessities, not
luxuries. Without them humanity cannot survive.* "
- Dalai Lama

In today's narcissistic, shopping-mad, celebrity-obsessed world, being better than others and having more than others, are qualities more revered than being a loving and compassionate human being. The root cause of our absurd behaviour is actually fear - fear of missing out, fear of what others think and fear of the hard work required to live a life of meaning. Most often this fear appears as disillusion, aimlessness and depression. Fear, at its darkest hour, can lead to homicide and suicide.

The opposite of this fear, is love, says Marianne Williamson. "Love is what we are born with. Fear is what we learn. The spiritual journey is the unlearning of fear and prejudices and the acceptance of love back in our hearts. Love is the essential reality and our purpose on earth. To be consciously aware of it, to experience love for ourselves and others, is the meaning of life. Meaning does not lie in things. Meaning lies in us."

Many of us today, are also suffering 'compassion fatigue' - a condition where our compassion is gradually lessened over time due to overexposure to the tragedies occurring around the world thanks to the media. We become de-sensitised and either totally turn-off or we develop an ever-increasing sense of hopelessness and helplessness. It's all we can do to muster up just enough love and compassion for those people closest to us: our partner, children, family and friends.

And most sadly, we show ourselves the least love and compassion. We, in fact, neglect and abuse ourselves the most.

> When work is done with love and compassion it doesn't even feel like work. It becomes as essential to daily life as breathing is to humans. It brings others joy. It heals the pain. It repairs and regenerates. It's of service to others.

So, how do you turn fear into love and compassion fatigue into compassionate action? You don't learn love and compassion from reading a book, watching TV or talking about the world's latest tragedy over dinner with your friends (although they're great for sparking ideas and generating action). You learn love and compassion through practising it, by willfully doing something that feels good to you and that serves others.

You start with yourself. You start with self-love and self-compassion. For many of us, that means surrendering first, the ultimate act of self-love. Then for each act of self-love, you offer an act of love to those you profess to love the most. You cook your family their favourite dinner. You commit to couples' therapy. You send a love letter. You give long, loving embraces. You tell your parents you love them, and you mean it.

Then you expand your love and compassion outside the confines of those you know intimately. You bring your love to work and beyond. You help a colleague with a serious deadline to meet. You have a compassionate conversation with a struggling co-worker. You give that homeless person your lunch. You volunteer at your kid's canteen. You greet the shop assistant with real care and warmth. You give a stranger an hour of your undivided attention. Then you think bigger. You think of the things that pain you most in your community, your company, your country or the world at large. You explore ways you can help and mobilise others to help. You volunteer for a charity, start a charity, donate to a charity.

You act on your love and compassion, because deeds speak far louder than words.

Love and compassion are the foundations for fulfilling your highest potential. When work is done with love and compassion it doesn't even feel like work. It becomes as essential to daily life as breathing is to humans. It brings others joy. It heals the pain. It repairs and regenerates. It's of service to others.

So, it seems, our purpose *is* love. Our purpose *is* compassion.

Love and compassion surely drove Mother Teresa and Mahatma Gandhi to live a life of service. I'm not suggesting we should all become Mother Teresa or Gandhi, but just imagine the world we'd live in, if we all just took one tiny leaf from their book. Wouldn't that be something?

According to the Guardian, in 2012, the most searched-for term on Google was, "what is love?" It seems that almost everyone is confused about this simple four-letter word!

Recently I decided to take on my own personal *Purpose Project* called 'The Love Project'. I've been exploring and experimenting with what romantic love actually means to me and what a fulfilling relationship might look like. I figure, if I apply the same diligence and focus to producing this book as I do to a relationship, then anything is possible!

Over the years, I've lost count of the number of well-meaning friends who've said, "love will happen when you least expect it and when you're not looking for it". Quite frankly, it's the biggest lie in the book. We wouldn't stand idly by and take such an apathetic approach to any other area of our life, so why would we apply it to our love life?

So many people have not taken seriously what may be the most important project of their life: to find and create a loving partnership. (If that's what you want, of course. Coupledom is not for everyone and I'm a big fan of the single-life and other forms of relationships too.) Many of us, however, have 'fallen into love' and coupled up with less consideration than we'd approach the buying of a car or house or where to holiday next.

And then, when we've found 'the one', we head into the abyss of the promised land of 'happily-ever-after' only to find ourselves seeking couples' therapy when things start to fall apart. Imagine a world where we all learnt what love really is and how to consciously choose a partner and create a healthy relationship before taking the plunge to coupledom.

For love to come to fruition, I must become a practitioner of love. I must take action because I don't want just any man (I've had that and it never ended well). I want someone I deserve and who is willing to go deep with me. That requires considered action, clearing of my old relationship-patterns, deep reflection on what I desire, lots of dates, new ways of stepping into and owning my divine femininity and sexuality, the resilience to face rejection and the foresight to reject those men not suitable.

First, however, I'm practising self-love and self-compassion as I know it's the only way to ultimately attract what I desire. Secondly, I'm practising on a daily basis how to extend my love and compassion to the beautiful people already in my life and to those I will never, ever get to meet that are suffering around the globe.

JESSICA'S STORY

When Jessica Smith was just three years old she recalls being dressed in a nurse's outfit at kindergarten and declaring to her buddies, "when I grow up I want to be a nurse that cares for kids".

She then went onto her local primary school in Templestowe and became, as she says, "an average student with average grades. I had no leadership positions and I didn't do anything very special. At the time, I just wanted to fit in". In 2013 when she was in year 7, her parents separated and her uncle passed away. It was pretty tough on her and her younger sister. "My sister had separation anxiety and would cry a lot. The teachers were great with her thankfully, but I don't think many teachers these days realise that students may just need a hug and someone to be kind to them."

Jessica is now a young woman aged 16 and a student at Templestowe College showing exemplary leadership with a real love and compassion for younger kids through her work on The Bridges Program. "My mum was always volunteering for things and helping others out, so I think some of her compassion for others must have rubbed off on me."

The Bridges Program brings students from Templestowe College to the nearby Templestowe Heights primary school. 25 kids, whose primary language is not English, are mentored to read by Jessica and three other permanent student workers with substitutes who fill in from time to time. Everyone works between 3-5 hours per week and is paid for their efforts. "I'm not only learning how to work with kids, I'm also learning how to run a business and manage staff," she says. "It's been an amazing experience and changed the way I think about the world and how I can help kids not as fortunate as me."

Sometimes the kids just don't want to read and they're distracted or troubled about something. That's when Jessica uses her true compassion. "I say... 'that's okay. What else do you want to do?' They want to go to the playground or just talk and be given a hug and have someone that will listen to them. They put so much trust in you. They really want to learn but they're dealing with stuff we have no idea about," says Jessica.

Out of school, Jessica spends a lot of time educating herself on world issues particularly those related to education and the environment. She watches documentaries and researches various issues facing children particularly in developing and war-torn countries. After school, Jessica intends to go to university to study teaching and then work with kids with disabilities, mental health issues and special needs.

"I want to work with the kids that fall through the cracks, the ones that need a teacher that can sit with them and help them through whatever they're going through," says Jessica. "While I'm not going to be a nurse that cares for kids, I've found my passion for teaching. I want to become a teacher that cares for kids instead."

Watch Jessica Smith's talk on The Slow School of Business YouTube channel.

TIME TO PRACTISE

Meditation & Reflection

Find a quiet spot where you'll be uninterrupted or go for a silent walk to reflect on the following scenarios. Do this exercise for at least 30 minutes while breathing fully into it. Try to drop into your body and your heart as much as possible and feel the answers and not over-think it.

Picture each of the people who are/were important to you in your life, including those who are no longer alive: your mother, father, children, siblings, partner, ex-partners, friends, ex-friends, co-workers. When you have an image of them in your mind, consider what that person may be dealing with in their life right now. Acknowledge their suffering.

Think of something you love about them. Breathe in and silently say this statement. "Dear Mum, I acknowledge that you are dealing with.... I love that you are..." As you breathe out say, "I offer you love and compassion. I wish you peace, health and happiness".

After you have done this, expand your thinking to imagine people you don't know that may be suffering: a homeless person, a refugee family, a child in slavery, a woman in a domestic violence situation, an elderly person with frail health, a man in deep depression. As you breathe in, breathe in their pain. As you breathe out say, "I offer you love and compassion. I wish you peace, health and happiness".

Finally bring back your attention to yourself and say the following, "Dear Me, I acknowledge that you are dealing with.... I love that you are..." As you breathe out say, "I offer you love and compassion. I wish you peace, health and happiness."

Then expand out this meditation to consider communities and countries of people living in poverty, pain, war and suffering. As you breathe in, breathe in their pain, as you breathe out say, "I offer you love and compassion. I wish you peace, health and happiness."

How will love and compassion help you to reach your highest potential?

Journaling Exercise	Now write for 30 minutes on the following: 1. Journal about all the answers to the questions in your meditation and reflection exercise. 2. How loving and compassionate are you in your daily life? (Rank 1-10: 1 being not at all, 10 being totally) 3. How loving and compassionate would you like to be? (Rank 1-10 as above) 4. What is the gap? Identify how large the gap is between questions 2 and 3. This will determine how much of a priority this practice is. 5. Set an intention for this practice. "I will practise more love and compassion by..." "I will know when I have fulfilled this intention when..."
Daily Practice	From the meditation and journaling exercise, identify at least one firm daily practice you will adopt to bring more love and compassion to your life, to work and others.
Big Action	Identify one big action you will take in the next week to shift your overall love and compassion factor up a whole notch. What is it? When will you do it?

PRACTICE 10
THE PRACTICE OF EMBRACING NATURE

Come forth into the light of things,
let nature be your teacher.
- William Wordsworth

There are really only two paths we can take in life. One path will lead us to finding more meaning and reaching our full potential, the other will divert us away from it.

One path is more akin to taking the multi-lane freeway, the one that the majority of humans take. It's the route that's most noisy and crowded and that will get you to your destination as quickly as possible. There are many signposts telling you exactly which town is next, how far you have to go and what speed to travel at. You can even calculate exactly when you'll arrive and pre-book the hotel and restaurant you'll be dining at. It's all very well thought-out and planned.

The second path, as M Scott Peck wrote, is "the road less travelled". This is more like a bumpy, deserted country dirt road with scant signage. You know your destination but you're not wedded to the time of arrival or where you'll settle for the night. The road has twists, turns and dead ends to navigate. It's all rather slow, adventurous and exquisite on the road less travelled!

As clichéd as this analogy is (sorry for that), the path to purpose is more akin to taking the country road than the freeway. It's where we're most present and paying attention. It's where anything is possible. The country road meanders its way through lush fields bearing gnarly old trees leading to gurgling creeks, wild oceans and barren plains. The country road opens us up to the natural world, for it's in our natural element that we truly find ourselves.

Just like nature, our life has seasons too. Sometimes we

Mother Earth has so much to teach us on our path to purpose. The travesty is that we're so disconnected from her that we don't receive the lesson.

need a winter of despair. Winter gives us a chance to bunker down, to hibernate then re-emerge with a new vision. We need the spring too. It's a time for planting new ideas, watering them and watching them grow. We need the summer for the long hot days of toiling and getting the work done and the autumn for shedding the stuff that's not working for us. And finally, we need the liminal states between the seasons, those times when we're not quite sure what's in store next. Each pleasurable, painful or in-between season passes as we continue down that glorious country road.

Mother Earth has so much to teach us on our path to purpose. The travesty is that we're so disconnected from her that we don't receive the lesson. We're simply not looking and we're not listening. Instead of learning from her, loving her and nurturing her, we're killing her, and in the process, we're killing ourselves.

We change this by wilfully surrendering to her. We stop. We sit. We breathe deeply. We meditate in her. We hear her cries for help. We whisper, we shout, we cry with love and compassion for her. We are not only at one with nature, we *are* nature. Then we commit to act. We reset the intentions for our life in deep consideration of our natural mother because she is, after all, our ultimate stakeholder.

The more you embrace Mother Earth, the more you'll awaken to your own innate natural state of being. You do this by scheduling regular outings in nature, either on your own or with your family. You walk barefoot on the grass and dig your toes into the dark brown earth. You start a local community vegetable garden. You clean your local parks and streets of rubbish. You reduce, reuse, refill, recycle and repair at home because you care what ends up in landfill. You plant edible gardens instead of lawn. You have a planter box of vegies on your balcony. You teach your kids where food comes from and show them how to grow it. You eat less meat or none at all. You shop wisely, because you know that each dollar you spend, is a vote for our planet.

When it comes to your workplace, you host conferences and events in the heart of our natural environment so your people can get plugged in to their deepest selves. You measure the negative impact of your company on the natural world and take measures to repair and regenerate it. You stand with your leadership team under an exquisite 200-year-old oak tree and listen deeply and compassionately to the wisdom this tree can impart to you and your company.

Mother Earth *is* our ultimate purpose. Without her, we are nothing. We become extinct.

Nature is playing an increasingly vital role in my daily life. I spend time in it every day, whether that's for a walk or a bike-ride along the river or meditating while sitting on a rock with the waters of the river swirling around me.

If my mind is racing with too many possibilities or I'm troubled about something, nature calls. I take a pillow, a blanket and my journal and spread out under a tree near the river and write, sometimes for pages and pages. In nature, I can breathe fully, listen deeply and think clearly. By the end I've always found the answers to my questions. I leave feeling at peace, clear-minded and resolved about the very next step to take.

In nature, I'm reminded that I'm small and insignificant in the big scheme of our great cosmos. I'm reminded that my problems are inconsequential. I'm reminded of how lucky I am, how grateful I am yet at the same time, how essential I am. In nature, I am in a state of bliss.

Every bird, every tree, every rock is a reminder of why I do what I do and it reinforces my commitment to keep showing up and doing the work. Nature inspires me to write, write and write some more.

As I'm more connected to the earth, I'm also increasingly aware of the impact my living and spending has on it. I'm becoming a more conscious consumer all round. I think twice about what I buy and who I buy it from and what part of my purchase might end up in landfill.

Mother Earth *is* our ultimate purpose. Without her, we are nothing. We become extinct.

Every day, I play a little game with myself and think up one new way to lighten my footprint or to get more connected to nature. I'm far from perfect, that's for sure and I can do much better, but it feels so good to be making gradual, mindful changes every day.

CLARE'S STORY

Clare Voitin and her husband, John, are the owners of Swan Bay Farm near Geelong and The Providore Swan Bay Farm in Balwyn, Melbourne. The Providore encourages people to buy and grow locally by showcasing the farm's produce and the artisan products and produce of other local growers.

After a frenetic week in the city, the family drives to the farm for the weekend. "The moment we enter the front gate, a deep sense of tranquillity overwhelms me. The slow switch is flicked on and I become a different woman," reflects Clare. "The farm is my place for mindfulness and writing (she is currently finishing her second book) and for getting my hands dirty tending to our gardens and animals. It's my creative haven and the place where I'm the happiest."

Clare and her sister grew up in the suburbs of Melbourne attending the local Catholic school. "We had a pretty humble, quite typical suburban life," says Clare. "Looking back on our childhood, I am very grateful for the uncomplicated upbringing that Mum and Dad gave us. We were provided with a safe, secure learning environment that taught us to appreciate the simple things and, in particular, enjoy a sense of freedom that today seems a challenge to pass on to our own children."

At the age of 10, Clare's parents took the family on a farming holiday. "I distinctly remember my fascination watching the shearers bring in the sheep to the shearing shed. There was an orphaned lamb sitting behind a log bleating and bleeding. Its mother had rejected her. I felt this overwhelming sense of sadness for it and I knew somehow that animals would play an important part in my life."

Clare's Dad was also an amateur gardener, always weeding, mowing the lawn around the Hills Hoist and tending his beloved vegie garden. "I'd help Dad in the garden quite a bit and we'd talk about everything and nothing. Looking back, this time together built a powerful connection between us, based simply on spending time together doing something that was important to him that would ultimately become incredibly important to me. This time together taught me a real appreciation for the earth and our natural world. I'd help dig, plant and water, but the best part was picking and eating what we'd produce. I had a real sense of pride in my efforts," says Clare.

These simple yet profound childhood experiences led Clare to where she is right now, living and working on one of her most fundamental reasons for being.

The family are fulfilling their dream to turn Swan Bay Farm into a place for education, awareness and connection. Their plans are to convert the farm into a place where families can come to dig, plant and learn about seasonal and organic produce, including heirloom produce. An apple museum has been planted, and a tomato museum is due for completion in the late spring.

Visitors will also get an insight into the support and care involved in the ethical raising of farm animals, as well as teaching simple ways to grow food organically. "We want to share information with others regarding our own farming practices in order to encourage others to have a go. We're proud of what we've achieved so far at Swan Bay Farm and we believe that opening our farm-gate to the public will give them a greater understanding of where their food comes from, how it's grown and raised and the process required in getting it from the paddock to the plate. It will also encourage people to support more ethical food production practices."

The best part for Clare and John is that their three boys aged 10, 12 and 14 absolutely love the farm and really appreciate the earth too. "They spend long days outdoors, exploring, playing, building treehouses and designing and constructing everything from chook sheds to sheep yards. They're learning about the cycle of life and death," reflects Clare. "Just like me as a child, they appreciate the benefits of growing and eating their own food. I want to provide an opportunity for parents and their kids to have access to the knowledge that we have."

In 2016, Clare completed the *Talk on Purpose* course. "I wish I'd done it 20 years ago," she said. "I had this 'ah-ha' moment that the businesses I run and the books I've written are all connected to my cause, which is to connect families to the earth and what they eat. I'm starting a good food movement here in Melbourne and my plan is to take it far and beyond!"

Watch Clare Voitin's talk on The Slow School of Business YouTube channel.

TIME TO PRACTISE

Meditation & Reflection	Find a quiet spot in nature where you'll be uninterrupted (it might be in your own garden or at a local park or while on a bushwalk). Do this exercise for at least 30 minutes while breathing fully into it. Try to drop into your body and your heart as much as possible and feel the answers and not over-think it.

Practise becoming aware of all the senses, one a time. First let your breath settle and notice your chest rising, your stomach expanding and contracting. Then tune into your sense of hearing. Notice the sounds closest to you then the sounds further away. Don't judge the sounds as good or bad, just listen.

Then tune into your sense of taste. Roll your tongue around your mouth, lick your lips, notice the taste. Then tune into your sense of smell. Breathe in deeply and identify the smells around you.

Then tune into your sense of touch. Notice what is touching your body, a breeze, the sun on your skin, your legs and feet on the ground, your fingers touching each other.

Next tune into your sense of sight. Open your eyes and look straight ahead, notice every single thing in front of you, every blade of grass, every leaf, every bird or ant, slowly turn your head and survey the scenes around you.

Finally, tune into your sixth sense, your extra-sensory perception. Elevate your thinking beyond what is around you to the whole world, the universe, what is above and beyond the landscape. In this place, just wonder. Let your mind imagine. Then bring it right back to your heart. Breathe in and out deeply three times.

What would a life deeply connected to nature look like for you? Describe a day in your life with nature infused in it. What would you be doing? Who would you be with? Where would you be? How would it impact your overall wellbeing and connection to self? How might nature help you to reach your highest potential?

Journaling Exercise	Now write for 30 minutes on the following:

1. Journal about all the answers to the questions in your meditation and reflection exercise.

2. How connected am I generally to nature?
    (Rank 1-10: 1 being not at all, 10 being totally)

3. How satisfying would it be, to be truly connected to nature?
    (Rank 1-10 as above)

4. What is the gap? Identify how large the gap is between questions 2 and 3. This will determine how much of a priority this practice is.

5. Set an intention for this practice.

    "I will practise embracing nature by..."
    "I will know when I have fulfilled this intention when..."

Simple Daily Practice	From the meditation and journaling exercise, identify at least one simple daily practice you will adopt to get more connected to nature in life and work.
Big Weekly Action	Identify one big action you will take in the next week to get more deeply connected to nature. What is it? When will you do it?

PRACTICE 11
THE PRACTICE OF BEING IN COMMUNITY

We have all known the long loneliness, and we have found that the answer is community.
- Dorothy Day

As we continue to do the purpose work, we may start to notice an increasing sense of disconnection from other people, even as we're sitting right amongst our fellow humans. We may go out to dinner with old friends and find the conversation boring. We may feel frustrated at the lack of conscious communication across our work team. We may notice some sadness as we find it impossible to engage our parents in a conversation that's deeper than the state of the weather. We may find that we feel lonelier in crowds than we do at home in solitude. We may feel, at times, that we simply don't belong.

Please know, all of this is okay. It's a really good sign. Don't judge yourself, or others for that matter. Just notice it, reflect on it and feel right into it. You're actually in the liminal state between the old and the new in terms of how you interact with people and how you wish your relationships to be. It's actually all solid affirmation that you're on the move, even though it's highly uncomfortable.

It's important to note that 'being alone' and 'being lonely' are not the same thing. Being alone is not the root cause of loneliness, being disconnected from what gives you real meaning is actually the root cause of loneliness. Learning how to be alone and loving it, is actually at the epi-centre of creating an expanded life, particularly if you're working on things you love.

As you shift out of your liminal state, you become more conscious about how you wish to spend time in relationship with others. Sometimes you're proactive and decide to end a destructive relationship. At other times, you choose to stay in a relationship with grace, yet with new boundaries that are acceptable to you. You review, refine or revoke your old relationships and you choose carefully your new relationships.

You'll also start to seek communities and people that share your new beliefs and values. Community is a word derived from 'common unity' which means that we are at one in our beliefs, vision or interests. The purpose of a community is to accomplish something that is meaningful to the community and important for the world, while enabling each individual to reach their highest potential. In community, you enter into communion with others who share the common goal. Community is where deep change is accelerated.

The more clarity you have about what really matters to you, the more likely it is that you'll find your tribe or find the impetus to build your own tribe. That's why you need to fully explore the ikigai purpose model and questions as you do this work. Joining a community (or starting your own), is a highly recommended great first *Purpose Project*. In community, you can co-create, co-own and co-activate solutions to problems and feel deeply fulfilled and alive.

You join a human rights community group. You get deeply immersed in a permaculture community. You join a dance, music or singing group. You start working at a co-working space with a bunch of clever humanistic creative souls. You go to festivals and workshops with people who share the same interests in advancing humanity. You start a food-share community group with your neighbours. You join a global online community championing suicide prevention. You join a charity that teaches young refugees how to read.

If you're an employee in a large company, you don't need to search outside to find your community. You can start right where you are and create your own special interest community inside your company. You create a yoga, meditation and

In community, you enter into communion with others who share the common goal. Community is where deep change is accelerated.

mindfulness community for employees and invite your clients to join in. You bring an art appreciation community to your workplace and invite artists in to speak and teach art at lunch times. You join the company's environmental community group, the bushwalkers group or the classical music appreciation group. You could even create your own *Purpose Project* community where people gather to do the purpose work each week.

Community is the elixir of life. It's the family of your choosing. It's like a coming home.

In 2001, when I simultaneously separated from my husband and left the corporate world to start my own business, I recall being overcome with a real sense of isolation as my social structures collapsed. I had no husband or family structure to rely on and no work place to belong to. My only friends had come from the corporate world while the world of small business was totally foreign to me. I was in transition between the old and the new and I didn't even know where to begin to find my new work tribe.

So, I started my own tribe. I found a couple of friends who were leaving the corporate world too and we started a networking group called *Connect Network* for freelance marketers, creatives, advertisers and more. For seven years, I ran and led the community and I absolutely loved it and I've been building communities ever since.

I get immense satisfaction out of being in common unity with others, connecting people and collaborating for change. Together we can do so much more than we can do alone. There's an African Proverb that says, "if you want to go fast, go alone. If you want to go far, go together". That to me, sums up exactly what community is all about.

As well as starting communities like *Slow School*, I've always loved being a part of other communities that are aligned with my values and philosophies, such as *Conscious Capitalism*, *B Corp* and the many co-working communities proliferating around the world.

I've learnt so much, and given and gained so much from community. This book, is in fact, the result of the collective wisdom of community.

IRMA & OLIVER'S STORY

In late 2002, Irma and Oliver Zimmermann moved from Switzerland to Melbourne with their two daughters, Gita and Tiana, aged 7 and 4. Irma was a self-employed graphic designer while Oliver found an IT job at one of Australia's largest insurance companies, IAG. "It was an exciting time. We were starting all over again. Our life was like a blank canvas to paint whatever we wanted on it," says Irma. "However, I wasn't expecting what happened next. We didn't know anyone in Melbourne and I had this really painful period of feeling disconnected and isolated from everyone back home and I got ill with chronic fatigue-like symptoms."

Irma worked hard to overcome her health problems by focusing on her family and business. At the same time, she recognised a gradual change in Oliver's demeanour. Usually a very sensitive, gentle and thoughtful man who would do anything for his family, she noticed he would often get angry, moody and defensive. "He became a different person at home to what everyone else saw. He hid it well, which made it difficult for me to share what was going on. My girlfriends would tell me to stop complaining and that I was lucky to have such a gorgeous husband which only made me feel more isolated. We were not alone but we were both lonely," says Irma.

As they were becoming so distant from each other, Irma insisted that they have couples counselling. The counsellor immediately identified that Oliver had depression. Oliver chose to deal with his depression naturally, through focusing on his health and exercise which included rekindling his passion for cycling.

In 2014, serendipity happened and life turned around for them both. Irma was at a conference and saw a speech by Peter Baines from Hands Across the Water. The charity provides homes for orphaned children in Thailand affected by the tsunami. Peter shared his story and invited the audience to participate in a 500-kilometre charity bike ride to raise funds for the orphanages. The goal was to raise $300,000 with a team of 45 people riding from Bangkok to Khao Lak, an hour and a half from Phuket on the western coast where the tsunami had hit. "I instantly felt a need to take action, so I signed up on the spot," laughs Irma. "I wasn't sure whether Oliver would join me, I just wanted to help and I didn't even own a bike!" Then as Irma started researching bikes, working out her training plan and asking for

Oliver's advice, Oliver became more and more engaged until one day he turned to Irma and said, "I want to do the ride too". "Immediately we had a common interest and a goal to achieve. We had to train together, keep each other motivated and work on our fundraising strategy. It connected us again and it was the catalyst for our healing and return to love," says Irma.

Now in 2017, they've just completed the bike ride for the third time and Irma is an ambassador for the charity. "We both love being a part of the Hands Family. There's a real sense of community amongst the riders, the kids in the orphanages and the people that run the orphanages," says Irma. "I'm also fascinated by the transformation that occurs with every single rider. They've all challenged themselves in one way or another – mentally and physically. We all come back more enriched, ready to live healthier lives and to make a difference."

Irma is also exploring how to use her newfound passions for bike riding, fitness and supporting less fortunate kids with her old talents in graphic design and online marketing. "I've been working with people that are purpose-driven in the areas of sport, fitness and personal development and am also working on a couple of my own projects aligned with my purpose. It's early days but I'm having lots of fun and gaining lots of insights by testing things out."

 Watch Irma and Oliver Zimmermann's talks on The Slow School of Business YouTube channel.

TIME TO PRACTISE

Meditation &   Find a quiet spot where you'll be uninterrupted. Do this exercise
Reflection   for at least 30 minutes while breathing fully into it. Try to drop
                   into your body and your heart as much as possible and feel the
                   answers and not over-think it.

                   Think about some of the recent events/occasions/community
                   groups and family gatherings you've been a part of. Choose one
                   where you felt disconnected or disassociated and one where
                   you felt really connected and plugged in.

                   First reflect on the event where you felt disconnected. What was
                   the purpose of the event? Why did you feel disconnected? Who
                   was there? What happened?

                   Put words to the feelings you had (sad, angry, distracted). What
                   was the root cause of this disconnection?

                   Next reflect on the occasion where you felt really connected.
                   What was the purpose of the event? Why did you feel
                   connected? Who was there? What happened?

                   Put words to the feelings you had (happy, loved, accepted).
                   What was the root cause of this connection?

                   Now consider what you stand for and what really matters to you.
                   Why do they matter? Who are the people, events, communities
                   that you want to experience more of, that make you feel
                   wholehearted and alive?

                   What would a strong sense of community look like for you?
                   Describe a day in your life where community has a significant
                   role to play. What would you be doing?

                   How would it impact your overall wellbeing? How will belonging
                   to a community help you to reach your highest potential?

Journaling Exercise	Now write for 30 minutes on the following:

1. Journal about all the answers to the questions in your meditation and reflection exercise.

2. How satisfied are you when it comes to your sense of belonging to community?
   (Rank 1-10: 1 being not at all, 10 being totally)

3. How satisfying would it be to belong to community?
   (Rank 1-10 as above)

4. What is the gap? Identify how large the gap is between questions 2 and 3. This will determine how much of a priority this practice is.

5. Set an intention for this practice.
   "I will practise being in community by..."
   "I will know when I have fulfilled this intention when..."

Simple Daily Practice	From the meditation and journaling exercise, identify one simple daily practice you will adopt to get more plugged into community.
Big Weekly Action	Identify one big action you will take in the next week to get more deeply connected into community/ies. What is it? When will you do it?

PRACTICE 12
THE PRACTICE OF LIVING SIMPLY

> *There are two ways to be rich. One is by acquiring much, and the other is by desiring little.*
> - Jackie French Koller

Sadly, human beings have made complexity, instead of simplicity, our default way of life. We've just accepted that in today's super-connected, super-consumptive world that complexity is normal and that we have no choice in the matter.

We make our lives complex in terms of how we use our time, our energy and our money. We fill our days with activities from the moment we wake up to the time we go to bed. While some of these activities are essential, many are often thoughtless and pointless. We find ourselves in back-to-back meetings during the day and, therefore, having to work at night. We find ourselves neglecting our health, our loved ones, our community because of the demands of others. When we do have free time, we spend it in shopping centres buying useless stuff that ends up in landfill and garage-fill. We have complex property portfolios propped up with huge piles of stressful debt. We have multiple bank accounts, credit cards, digital devices, social media platforms, properties and cars. We have wardrobes bulging with clothes, yet nothing to wear!

We're both pathological consumers of stuff and pathological consumers of time. Complexity and busyness are great partners and they're actually the symptoms of disconnection from self. They're an addiction that is no different to alcohol and drug addiction. They keep us numb and distracted and diverted away from what really matters.

Complexity results in a contracted life. Simplicity, on the other hand, results in an expanded life. Fools create complexity, while geniuses remove it.

One reason many of us don't fulfil our dreams is because we haven't created the time and space required to dedicate ourselves to the

> Complexity results in a contracted life. Simplicity, on the other hand, results in an expanded life. Fools create complexity, while geniuses remove it.

pursuit of the dream. Instead of removing things from our complex and busy lives to create that space, we pile the dream on our junk-heap of forgotten dreams and our already over-burdened lives.

There's no way you can fulfil your calling if you don't have the head-space, heart-space and time-space to make it happen.

Today, there's a growing 'minimalism' movement erupting across the globe. Minimalism is all about freeing ourselves from our manic desire to possess and consume. It's about living simply with the essentials and taking the 'less is more' approach.

To practice the art of living simply, you must first notice and surrender to the complexity and busyness of your life. You become aware of what's complex and causing you stress and what's simple and bringing you joy. You start by simplifying the way you live on a daily basis. You assess how you spend your time and money and what should stay or go. Each time you do something or buy something, you ask yourself, "is this in alignment with my highest intention?"

As you simplify, you're careful not to fill the space that's been created with other complex stuff. You keep the space sacred and use it to work on your pet *Purpose Project.*

We each have the power to simplify our life in a way that works best for us. The timing might be right to downsize your home and eliminate your debt. You might change your work habits to free up time to prioritise your project. It may involve amalgamating, reducing and simplifying your banking or reducing your wardrobe items to no more than you need for a week of wearing. It may involve cleaning out your home and office and giving your stuff away to those who need it more than you. You might establish a manifesto for your household around living simply with less, so that you can all *be* more. You could analyse your spending and redirect the money you spend on stuff towards an experience that is good for you and good for the world.

From a place of simplicity, you're able to gain greater clarity around your intentions. You make these intentions few and laser-sharp focused.

To live simply is to be free.

Last year, I downsized and minimalised my life. I sold my home, eliminated my debt, moved into a rental apartment half the size and bought a new apartment in a like-minded 'small footprint' community near nature (now being built). In the process, I reduced my possessions by about half.

Today, my money and time is spent on experiences not things: writing, reading, nature, dance, walking, travel, music, family and friends and supporting the few communities that I belong to.

Living minimally has unburdened me and created the space to focus whole-heartedly on my business intentions, which are to increase the impact and scale of *The Purpose Project* not only in Australia, but in the US and other countries too.

My other two intentions around health and love are also really starting to pay off as I've created the space to devote to them. Each time I'm about to spend time or money on something or when an opportunity presents itself, I ask myself, "Is this action or opportunity going to take me closer to achieving one of my intentions? If so, how? If not, say NO!"

A year or two ago, I had a far more complex and cluttered life. Today, I consciously choose to have less and be more. For me, it's the best way to make shift happen towards my calling.

Now, I realise that my approach is not for everyone. It works for me right now, because of my stage in life and because it's deeply aligned with my highest values and beliefs. Also, I'm not advocating austerity, I'm advocating simplicity so that you are free to play and create whatever your heart desires.

BROOKE'S STORY

Brooke McAlary and her husband, Ben, live with their two kids and their dog and chooks in the Blue Mountains just outside Sydney, Australia.

In 2010, while heavily pregnant with her second child, renovating their home and running her jewellery business, Brooke had a breakdown. "My Mum and

Ben got me through it and after Toby was born I was diagnosed with post-natal depression. I'd had it since my first child was born but it hadn't been diagnosed. I just thought it was normal to feel like that after giving birth," says Brooke. "I distinctly remember a moment when we were on holidays in Canada and I was reading this book that was full of questions to journal on. I was asked to write my own eulogy in a sentence and imagine my kids were reading it at my funeral. I wrote 'Mum, thank you for our roots and our wings'."

In that moment Brooke had a rude moment of awakening and she felt forlorn and deeply depressed. "I realised that while I had a desire to live an adventurous, spontaneous, creative life that would be good for me and my family, I was actually living a self-centred, introspective, moody life. I wasn't behaving or living in a way that would enable my kids to feel like they had roots and wings."

At the time, Ben was commuting to the city every day for work while Brooke was running the family home, her business and looking after the kids. "I was trying to live up to this ideal of being a woman that had it all, but I was completely beside myself and overwhelmed. I don't remember being happy. I was always thinking about the next thing to do. Life became transactional and there was little joy," says Brooke.

Brooke went to a psychiatrist who questioned her about her lifestyle, her home, how she filled her time and what was important to her. She put her onto the idea of living simply. "I got home and googled 'how to simplify my life' and found the *Zen Habits*. I just read everything I could on the subject of living with less and doing less. Then Ben and I started to gradually simplify and declutter our life. I closed my jewellery business. We decluttered the house, the drawers, the cupboards and the kids toy boxes. We got rid of all the useless stuff that was sitting in our double garage that was weighing us down. Then we flattened the garage and created a vegetable garden in its place."

Over time Ben and Brooke were able to reconnect and rebuild their life around what was important to their family with 'living simply' being their mantra. As Brooke started to heal, she noticed more and more people being interested in her journey and how she was creating a simple life for her family. This led to the creation of their radio station, JackRabbit.FM and *The Slow Home Podcast* which has had more than two million listeners in the two years it's been running.

When asked what the relevance of living simply is to finding purpose, Brooke answers very clearly. "We don't realise how heavy our stuff is. Stuff keeps us feeling obligated and guilty. It weighs us down emotionally. Actively and intentionally letting go of our belongings releases mental energy and helps us gain clarity. We start to rethink our role as a consumer and we have more freedom."

Out of the ashes, the phoenix rises. Today Brooke has turned her personal travesty into triumph and she's now living a wholehearted, happy life pursuing her passion.

 Listen to Brooke McAlary interview Carolyn Tate on The Slow Home Podcast.

TIME TO PRACTISE

Meditation & Reflection	Do this walking reflection exercise for at least 30 minutes while breathing fully into it. Try to drop into your body and your heart as much as possible and feel it and not over-think it.
	Walk around your home and notice the stuff you have and own. Open the drawers, look in your cupboards, visit your garage. Don't just superficially scan it all, look at every single thing, touch it, notice it and reflect on how and when it was used and its importance in your life. Leave no drawer unturned. Just feel into it.
	Then take a seat and think of all the projects, activities, obligations you have in your life. Just feel into them, no need to write them at this stage. What are all the things you own (or that own you)? Think of everything you own or have to manage i.e. bank accounts, properties, cars and so on.
	Then grab your journal and a pen and take 3 deep breathes. Write a list of every single thing you can think of that you own and are responsible for in your life. Once you've done that reflect on how you feel about this list of things. Do you feel at ease with it? Do you feel happy and joyful about this list? Or do you feel burdened, overwhelmed, angry and annoyed? Just sink into the feeling you have about it all.
	Don't judge how you feel, just feel it. What specific things on this list are enabling or derailing you in your shift towards your calling? What would living simply look like for you? Describe a day in your life of simple living. What would you be doing? How would it impact your overall wellbeing? How might living more simply enable you to reach your highest potential? What do you need to do now to live more simply?

Journaling Exercise	Now write for 30 minutes on the following:
	1. Journal about all the answers to the questions in your meditation and reflection exercise.
	2. How satisfied are you with your practice in living simply? (Rank 1-10: 1 being not at all, 10 being totally)
	3. How satisfying would it be to live more simply? (Rank 1-10 as above)
	4. What is the gap? Identify how large the gap is between questions 2 and 3. This will determine how much of a priority this practice is.
	5. Set an intention for this practice. "I will practise living simply by..." "I will know when I have fulfilled this intention when..."
Simple Daily Practice	From the meditation and journaling exercise, identify one simple daily practice you will adopt to live more simply.
Big Weekly Action	Identify one big action you will take in the next week to live more simply. What is it? When will you do it?

REVIEWING YOUR PRACTICES

 If you always do what you've always done, you'll always get what you've always got.
- Henry Ford

As I said in the introduction to this part of the book, we only discover our passion by connecting with the parts of ourselves that have been asleep. We do this by seeking new experiences outside our day-to-day duties and routines. We practise new ways of being and behaving in our daily lives, and then we observe and take notice of what's working for us and what's not. It requires courage to fully embrace the purpose practices and go on this journey. We must, however, become daily practitioners of purpose. Please don't stop here. Keep going!

Now that you've completed all the exercises, review your journal to reaffirm for yourself the activities you've committed to on a daily or weekly basis.

Once you've done the exercise below, it's onto the final part of this book, where you get to set your *Purpose Project/s* (if you haven't already jumped ahead and done that!).

> We only discover our passion by connecting with the parts of ourselves that have been asleep. We do this by seeking new experiences outside our day-to-day duties and routines.

Allow yourself a good two or three hours to do this task.

Grab your journal and a highlighter pen.

Go through each of the 12 practices and review everything you've written and highlight the words, phrases and activities that stood out for you.

Review the intention you set for each practice. How are you going with those intentions? (If you're not going so well, please don't judge yourself).

What do you need to recommit to and do? Put tasks in your diary to refocus on specific practices. Make a commitment to review your practices each week for 30 minutes.

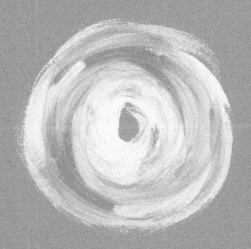

PART 5

CREATING YOUR
PURPOSE PROJECT

WHY PURPOSE PROJECTS?

> *It takes half your life before you discover that life is a do-it-yourself project.*
> - Napoleon Hill

Yes, you've already read this quote in this book. In my view, it's a quote really worth repeating! Napoleon Hill was the author of *Think and Grow Rich*, and it's the book that I'm re-reading right now. This all-time classic, first published in 1937, has sold millions of copies around the world. The book offers 13 proven steps to turn your desire into riches. While very masculine in its language, it's well worth reading as I believe it's the perfect companion and sequel to *The Purpose Project*.

The first step in *Think and Grow Rich* is 'desire'. The author states that desire (knowing exactly what we want) is the starting point of all achievement. Maybe he assumes (or hopes) that readers actually know *what* they desire and *why* they desire it.

In my opinion, the reason many of us don't find riches or prosperity, is because we truly don't know what we desire. We've been conditioned to view 'desire' as the fulfilment of our superficial, shallow wants rather than the fulfilment of our deep, intrinsic calling.

If we don't know the *why* behind our desire, then it will be tough to bring it to life.

In the beginning of this book, I shared my philosophy on why I believe we should adopt *Purpose Projects* in our work (and life). Projects

Action precedes clarity, right? How do you know if you're on the right path unless you give something a go and try it out? We learn best by doing.

are a great way to test, prototype and experiment to work out whether our new direction is truly what we desire. Action precedes clarity, right? How do you know if you're on the right path unless you give something a go and try it out? We learn best by doing.

The ultimate goal of this book is to help you pick a project that will help you do that. The project will help you accomplish something that makes the most of your skills and talents and that is meaningful to you and the world beyond yourself.

You can adopt *Purpose Projects* within your current work place. You can adopt them outside of work while you're still doing your day job and then you might explore ways to integrate them into your work. You can create a portfolio livelihood of projects that occur simultaneously or sequentially. You can take on a *Purpose Project* to test whether you should be investing in a university course or some other long term education program. *Purpose Projects* can also be undertaken in all other areas of our life too, in the areas of love, health, charity, community, family and more.

One reason projects fail before they even get started, is that we lack the courage and the curiosity to step over that first threshold and do something radically different that will kick-start the project. You will not unleash your passion unless you get uncomfortable and step outside of the conditioned patterns of behaviour that have kept you stuck. It requires you to hold your breath and just do it no matter how excruciatingly scary it might be for you. As Martin Luther King Jr said, "you don't need to see the whole staircase, you just need to take the first step".

Another reason projects fail is that we give up too soon if it doesn't 'feel right' at first attempt. We don't have the fortitude or commitment to stick to our promises and give the project enough time to gain momentum and traction. We don't test things out thoroughly enough or gather the essential data and evidence on which to make robust decisions about the next steps with our project. We must do, then test and then rinse and repeat.

And a final reason a project may fail is all to do with this riddle: "How do you eat an elephant?" The answer: "one bite at a time!" Many of us are so impatient that we attempt to eat the whole elephant at once or we bite off more than we can chew and we choke. We make the project too big and seemingly too impossible so we end up aborting it. That's why I'm a big proponent of starting with small, short, achievable projects. We approach purpose bite by bite.

Purpose Projects should work in stages and as building blocks to work towards your bigger, higher calling. As an example, imagine you're an employee at a large corporation and you work in a team of 20 people. You're passionate about meditation and mindfulness, so you create your own purpose statement around this. You then develop a small 3-month project to bring mindfulness into meetings and you offer daily meditations for those people interested at a certain time each day. Then once this project is embraced by your team, you teach others to run the meditation sessions and so on. There's a myriad of possibilities on how this project could be expanded on and have a ripple effect across the company.

What's your project going to be? What will you take a big leap of faith on and bring to life?

SCOPING YOUR PURPOSE PROJECT

> *Inspiraction [noun]: An emotionally and/or spiritually inspired idea that compels one to take action without delay. Otherwise known as 'inspired action'.*
> - Carolyn Tate

Remember that word inspiraction? Now's the time to tap into it.

By now you should have some idea on what your *Purpose Project* will be. I truly do hope so!

Believe me, once you know what your project is and once you become so convicted of it and start to take action, synchronicity will occur.

There are some important parameters to set before getting started so you can be sure that your project is truly important to you and so that it will come to fruition. Remember you must know the *what* and the *why* and let the *how* unfold a little more loosely. You're like a horse on a race track without blinkers so you can see what's going on all around you and seize the opportunities that arise during the race.

Believe me, once you know what your project is and once you become so convicted of it and start to take action, synchronicity will occur.

The following questions will help you scope out your *Purpose Project* and set parameters for it:

1. What is your *Purpose Project?* What do you want to achieve?
    (Write a statement of what the project is, e.g. I will test the viability of doing a degree in anthropology. I will hold my own photographic exhibition. I will...)

2. Why is this project important to you?
    (The answer to this will reveal just how committed you are. Would you die for it?)

3. What is the worst-case scenario if you don't fulfil your *Purpose Project?*
    (Get dramatic. Would you die if it's not fulfilled?)

4. What does your life look, feel, taste, sound, smell like as you are fulfilling your project? (Where will you be? Who with? Doing what? How will you feel?)

5. What do you need to give up in order to bring your project to life?
    (What holds you back? What projects/habits/people/activities do you need to stop so you have the space to achieve your intention?)

6. Which of the 12 purpose practices are most important to adopt in helping you achieve this *Purpose Project?*
    (Review the practices and choose the most important intentions.)

7. Who is going to be impacted by your project? How will they be impacted?
    (Family, clients, employees, co-workers, suppliers, society, environment)

8. What are the daily promises you make in fulfilling your project?
    (What are the habits I need to adopt day-in-day-out?)

9. What are the first three steps you need to take to start fulfilling your project?
    (Doing research, booking a class, writing a short action plan?)

10. Who can help you fulfil your project?
    (Who do you need to engage to help you on this journey? Suppliers, partners, funders, coach, family?)

11. How will you know when you have fulfilled your *Purpose Project?* (What will you have achieved? How will you be feeling? What will others say?)

12. What are the milestones you will set for this project? (What are the stepping stones, dates, measurements to establish?)

13. What structures and support systems do you need to put in place/use to ensure you achieve this project? (Use of diary, daily reminders, goal setting app, recording notes etc.)

Set aside at least four hours to do this exercise.

Go back through your journal from day one when you started and review where you were and where you are now.

Review the *Statement of Intention* you set for yourself. How have you gone on that?

Review the 12 practices and your intention statements. Which ones are most important to you?

Finally identify a *Purpose Project* that you would like to pursue.

Answer all the questions on the previous page and scope out the project in detail.

Go to your diary and set up the activities and times required to take action for the next month. Develop a simple project plan for yourself.

Now is the time to bring your *Purpose Project* to life. It's time to complete your plan, set aside the time, gather the resources, the people and the courage to take the first step. It's time to take the first bite out of the elephant! Have you found your mastermind group? Do you have a purpose buddy? Have you gathered a handful of conscious co-workers to work on this with? Whatever you need to do, just do it. You have everything you need to start right now, you truly do. You don't need to wait for permission from anyone. The only permission you need is your own. Ready? Go!

CONCLUSION

" Until one is committed, there is hesitancy, the chance to draw back, always ineffectiveness. Concerning all acts of initiative and creation, there is one elementary truth the ignorance of which kills countless ideas and splendid plans: that the moment one definitely commits oneself, then providence moves too.

All sorts of things occur to help one that would never otherwise have occurred. A whole stream of events issues from the decision, raising in one's favour all manner of unforeseen incidents, meetings and material assistance which no man could have dreamed would have come his way.

Whatever you can do or dream you can, begin it. Boldness has genius, power and magic in it. Begin it now. "

\- Johann Wolfgang von Goethe

Somewhere back in the dim dark ages of my youth, I seem to recall having a real love of dancing, mainly just at parties or concerts, nothing formal. And then somehow over time, I gradually lost that love and I didn't even realise it. I don't think I've danced for at least ten years!

Earlier this year, I plucked up the courage to attend my first ever dance class. This class had few rules, no formal steps to follow and no partners. The one rule was that you must not speak. For two hours, you're invited to drop into your body and right into the music and dance like no one's watching (which they aren't!).

The moment I stepped onto the dance floor amongst the 200 or so very cool and breezy dancers, I felt like Alice in Wonderland falling down the rabbit hole. It felt mighty uncomfortable and scary as I began to sway to the music. My self-doubt and self-judgement kicked in from the first move. "I can't dance. I look stupid. They'll laugh at me. What if someone tries to dance with me? Why, oh, why did I decide to do this? This is the first and last time I do this!" And on and on the negative self-talk went for the first hour of the class.

Then something really strange happened. I got out of my head and let my body fully surrender to the music. It carried me into a state of pure bliss. By the end of the class, I was totally sweaty, happy and hooked! The class has now become an essential part of my weekly regime. And the knock-on effect has been exquisite. It's inspired me to attend more dance and live music events and it's improved the way I write and speak. It's made me freer, more heart-driven and vulnerable. I'm committed to expanding this area of my life in service to the fulfilment of my *Purpose Projects.*

So why am I telling you this story? Remember the story of the Golden Buddha? I had to remove the layer of clay that had prevented me from unearthing my latent love of dancing. I had to return to my golden intent and reconnect with my essence. This required both courage and commitment.

Courage is the most essential quality required to take that first step onto the dance floor of purpose, while it takes real commitment to stay there. Without courage and commitment, you'll remain forever ineffective and diverted away from fulfilling your highest potential.

What do you need to find the courage for? What's your commitment to bringing meaning to life at work? What's your *Purpose Project* going to be?

It's time to unearth your Golden Buddha and step onto your own dance floor of purpose, starting right where you are, right now, with all that you have.

Courage is the most essential quality required to take that first step onto the dance floor of purpose, while it takes real commitment to stay there. Without courage and commitment, you'll remain forever ineffective and diverted away from fulfilling your highest potential.

If not you, who? If not now, when?

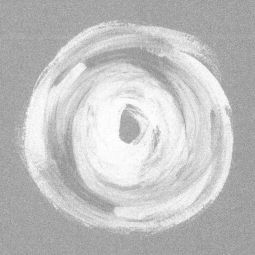

INDEX

1 Million Women...98
12-step group...12, 132
750 Words...15
About the author...x
Acknowledgements...xii
AFR...x
Agreement, acquiescence, activism...79
Aix-en-Provence, France...3, 167, 180, 220
Alcoholics Anonymous...132
Ali, Muhammad...165
Alice in Wonderland...209
Aligned for Life...134
American School in London...39
AMP Amplify...168
Anaïs Nin...125
Anear, Luke...100
Angelou, Maya...125
Apple...83
Ashe, Arthur...68
Athenaeum Theatre...61
Atlassian...88, 98
Australia Ballet School...135
Automation...33
AVAAZ...33
Baines, Peter...188
Bieber, Justin...25
BKindred...155
Bombeck, Irma...104
Branson, Richard...21
Brazille, Donna...107

Bright Shiny Object Disorder (BSOD)...159
Brown, Brené...109
BRW...x
Bukowski, Charles...138
BYO Purpose...94, 105
Cameron, Julia...5,165
Campbell, Joseph...21
Cardiff Business School...122
Carr-Gregg, Michael Dr...141
Carlisle, Thomas...166
Carolyn Tate & Co....x, 5, 88
Carrey, Jim...29
Carrots and sticks...93
Carson, Andre...95
Certified B Corporation...x, 187
Charity...23, 57, 77, 81, 172
Clarity of purpose...13, 14, 42, 85
Co-operative...33, 77, 83
Cohen, Leonard...iv
Collective Purpose...22, 90, 92, 101
Commercial Bank of Australia...4
Commitment...44, 204, 210
Compassion fatigue...171
Conclusion...209
Confucius...45, 85
Connect Network...187
Connect with Carolyn...220
Conscious Capitalism...x, 122, 139, 140, 187
Conscious Marketing...x, 5, 127, 140, 219

Conscious Marketing
    Revolution...127
Corporate escapees...10, 70, 92
Corporate services...218
Courage factor...126
Courageous conversation...79
Creating your Purpose Project...201
    Why Purpose Projects? ...203
    Scoping your Purpose
        Project...206
    Conclusion...209
Creativity definition...165
Culture programs...10, 103
Dalai Lama...74, 171
Damon, William...22, 152
Day, Dorothy...185
Dedication...iii
Deepwater Horizon...101
Defining purpose...22
    higher purpose...24
    organisational purpose...80
Desire...203
Discovering your personal work
    purpose...13, 49
    Finding your work purpose...51
        Unearthing your Golden
            Buddha...51
    Discover your ikigai...54
        Ikigai purpose model...55
        What you can be paid
            for...55
        What you are good at...56
        What you love...56
        What the world needs...56
        What circles are you working
            in?...57
    Laura's story...59
    Your 50 Purpose Questions...61
        A word of warning before
            you start...62

50 questions...63-67
    Start where you are...68
    Karen's story...70
    The signs of purpose...72
    Become a Purpose Activist...74
Dyer, Wayne...43
Edison, Thomas...139
Einstein, Albert...72
Etsy...83, 98
Evernote...15
Facebook...83
Firms of Endearment, Raj
    Sisodia...139
Fitted for Work...5
For-profits (FPs)...81
Ford, Henry...146, 198
Frankl, Victor...27, 54
Freeman, Ed...77
French Koller, Jackie...192
Freud...144
Frost, David...151
Fuller, Buckminster...6
Gallup Poll...7, 79
Gandhi, Mahatma...144, 173
Get Up...98
Getting started on purpose...13, 19
    What is purpose?...21
        Defining purpose...22
        The fluidity of purpose...23
        Defining 'higher
            purpose'...24
        Another word for
            purpose...25
    The history of purpose
        (lessness)...27
        The industrial age killed
            purpose...28
        Parents & the education
            system killed purpose...29
    The future of purpose...31

Our needs have evolved...31
The world of work has evolved...32
Technology enables higher purpose...33
Purpose drives prosperity...35
Our money mind-set...35
Cultivating a prosperity mind-set...36
Robert's story...38
The Purpose Project...40
The what & why...41
Setting your intention...43
Give yourself permission...43
Writing your statement of intention...45
From intention to action...47
Gibran, Khalil...7
God...24, 121, 133
Golden Buddha...51-53, 92, 97, 152, 210
Green-washing...78
Gross Domestic Product (GDP)...28
Gross National Happiness, GNH), Bhutan...28
Guardian...173
Guiding north-star...23, 55, 80, 86
Hands Across the Water...189
Harvard Business Review/ Ernst & Young Beacon Institute...10, 77
Herald-Sun...x
Hill, Napoleon...40, 203
Hitnet...98
Holstee Manifesto...109
Hudson, Jennifer...61
Human needs & personal motivation model...32
Human rights...6
Humanist...8, 74, 92

Ikigai...13, 25, 54-62, 93, 155, 163, 186
Industrialisation...7, 28
Inspiraction...14, 206
Interface Carpets...98
International Bilingual School of Provence...4
Intrinsic motivation...10, 24, 92, 203
Introduction...1
My purpose journey...3
Why we need this book...6
Who this book is for...9
A note for business leaders & employees...10
A note for entrepreneurs, start-ups & small business owners...11
A note for students, educators & parents...11
A note for couples & families...12
How to use this book...13
A handbook & a course...13
The power of journaling...15
Taking an active approach...14
Setting up the foundations...15
JackRabbit.FM...195
Jennings, Beth...xii
Jobs, Steve...54
Johns Hopkins University...27
Journaling...15
KeepCup...98
Kennedy, JF...51, 92
Key performance indicators (KPIs)...70
Kinfolk Café...154
Learn-by-doing...11, 12, 139, 140, 155

Learning Manifesto...109
Lennon, John...24
LGBTQI rights...6, 129
Liberating the Corporate Soul,
    Richard Barrett...31
Logo-therapy...27
Lululemon manifesto...109
Mackey, John...140
Maharishi University of
    Management...29
Man's Search for Meaning, Victor
    Frankl...27, 28
Mandela, Nelson...169
Marketing Manifesto...109
*Marketing your Small Business for
    Dummies*...x
Maslow's Hierarchy of Needs...31
Mastermind group...16, 45, 47, 118,
    139, 168, 208
Merrill Lynch...4
Minimalism movement...193
Mother Earth...6, 8, 179
Mother Teresa...173
Mount Gambier, South Australia...4
Multiple Possibility Disorder
    (MPD)...159
Not-for-profits (NFPs)...81
Novogratz, Jacqueline...81
Optus...83
Other books by Carolyn...221, 222
Patagonia...83, 98
Path to Purpose, William Damon...22
Pauling, Linus...158
Peck, M Scott...178
Pele...117
Peppermint Magazine...x
Permission slip...44
Picasso, Pablo...21
Pilates...134

Portfolio livelihoods...32, 69,
    135, 204
Prosperity-driven...82
Purpose Activists...iiv, 10, 74, 79, 92,
    107, 112
Purpose
    Purpose drives prosperity...35
    Purpose buddy...16
    Purpose definition...22
    Purpose economy...36
    Purpose effect...107
    Purpose experience...78
    Purpose health-check...104
    Purpose movement...79, 92
    Purpose promise...78
    Purpose-driven...82
    Purpose statements...98
    Purpose-washing...78
Raison d'être...4, 25, 72, 77, 85, 95
Rao, Srikumar...31
Rattigan, Marlene...xii
Real Women...167
Rohn, Jim...16, 112
RVLoveTV...162
RV Success School...162
Self-leadership...9, 10, 68, 70
Serenity Prayer...120
Shakespeare, William...70
Sinek, Simon...25, 102
Slow Living...x
Small Business Big Brand...x
sparks & honey...169
Stafford, Billy...x, xii, 3-4, 122,
    128, 146
Statement of Intention...45-47, 67,
    113, 208
Start with Why, Simon Sinek...25
Steinem, Gloria...3
Stocksy...83
Swan Bay Farm...181

Talk on Purpose...x, xii, 5, 154
TED talks...25
TEDx...39, 140
Templestowe College...98, 140, 174
Tesla...83, 87
The Age...x
The Art Below Summer Show...39
The Artist's Way, Julia Cameron...5
The Barrett Values Centre...88
The Beautiful Question...61
The Business Case for Purpose...10, 77
The Change School...139
The Golden Handcuffs...151
The Hub...140
The Human Age...iv, 6, 31
The Power of Now, Eckhart Tolle...146
The Providore...181
The School of Life...139
The School of Philosophy...80, 140
The Slow Home Podcast...195
The Slow School of Business...x, xii, 5, 80, 139, 140, 153, 187
The Soul of Money, Lynne Twist...37
Think and Grow Rich, Napoleon Hill...203
Thoreau, Henry David...38, 58
ThoughtWorks...87
Time to Think, Nancy Klein...61
Tolle, Eckhart...119
Top 5 Regrets of the Dying, Bronnie Ware...125
Twain, Mark...21
Tzu, Lao...9
Uber...83
Ueshiba, Morihei...109
ULab...139
Unearthing the purpose of your organisation...13, 75

The purpose of your enterprise...77
    The imperative of purpose...77
    Defining organisational purpose...80
The prosperity-driven enterprise...81
    The Profit-for-Purpose Enterprise Model...82
Purpose. Vision. Mission. Values...85
    The P.V.M.V. Model...86
    Purpose...86
    Vision...87
    Mission...87
    Values...88
The 3 levels of purpose...90
    The 3 Levels of Purpose model...90
    Higher purpose...91
    The collective purpose...92
    BYO Purpose...92
The (higher) purpose statement...95
    The purpose statement framework...96
    Examples of great purpose statements...98
SafetyCulture's story...100
Telstra's story...102
The purpose health-check...104
    The purpose health-check questions...105
The purpose effect...107
The manifesto...109
    The manifesto model...111
It's up to you...112
Unstuck in Provence...x, 5, 121, 128, 220

von Goethe, Johann Wolfgang...209
Wake Up Project...98
Walsch, Neale Donald...43
Westpac...4
Wheatley, Margaret...90
Whole Foods Market, John
    Mackey...140
Whyte, David...61
Wikileaks...33
Wikipedia...83
Wilde, Oscar...5
Williamson, Marianne...171
Women's March...6
Women's rights...6
Wordsworth, William...178
Zen Habits...195
Zimmermann, Irma...xii

The Purpose Stories
    Annalie Killian's story...168
    Beth Jennings story...147
    Billy Stafford's story...128
    Brooke McAlary's story...194
    Carolyn Tate's story...3
    Clare Voitin's story...181
    Irma and Oliver Zimmermann's
        story...188
    Jessica Smith's story...174
    Julie and Marc Bennett's
        story...161
    Karen's story...70
    Katrina Edwards story...134
    Laura's story...59
    Matt Perfect's story...122
    Penny Locaso's story...154
    Peter Hutton's story...140
    Robert Davis' story...38
    Rosa's story...93
    SafetyCulture's story...100
    Telstra's story...102

The 12 Practices of Purpose...13, 115
    Introducing the 12 practices...117
    Practice 1: The practice of
        surrendering...119
    Practice 2: The practice of finding
        courage...125
    Practice 3: The practice of self-
        care...131
    Practice 4: The practice of re-
        learning...138
    Practice 5: The practice of
        becoming conscious...144
    Practice 6: The practice of
        redefining success...151
    Practice 7: The practice of
        curiosity...158
    Practice 8: The practice of
        creativity...165
    Practice 9: The practice of love &
        compassion...171
    Practice 10: The practice of
        embracing nature...178
    Practice 11: The practice of being
        in community...185
    Practice 12: The practice of living
        simply...192
    Reviewing your practices...198

Purpose exercises and practices
    Finding your work purpose...53
    Give yourself permission...44
    It's up to you...113
    Karen's story...71
    Purpose drives prosperity...37
    Purpose. Vision. Mission.
        Values....89
    Scoping your purpose
        project...207, 208
    Statement of Intention...46-47
    The 3 Levels of Purpose...94

The 12 Practices of Purpose
    Time to practise...124, 130,
        136, 142, 149, 156, 163,
        170, 176, 183, 191, 196
    Reviewing your
        practices...199
The (higher) purpose
    statement...99
The prosperity-driven
    enterprise...84

The purpose effect...108
The purpose health-check...05,
    106
The manifesto...110
What is purpose?...26
Your 50 Purpose
    Questions...63-67

CONNECT WITH CAROLYN

Get more stories, free tools and live updates:

RESOURCES	Read Carolyn's blogs and interviews and download reading lists, tools and research at her website. **www.carolyntate.co**
SUBSCRIBE	Subscribe to Carolyn's fortnightly email updates to read more stories of purpose-driven people. **www.carolyntate.co**
FACEBOOK	Watch her facebook live sessions and interviews with purpose-driven leaders and get access to more tools and stories. **@carolyntateco**
TWITTER	Join the conversation on Twitter and keep up to date on the latest news and events. **@carolyntateco**
YOUTUBE	Watch the *Talk on Purpose* stories featured in this book and subscribe to *The Slow School of Business* YouTube channel.
SLOW SCHOOL	Find out more about *The Slow School of Business* and subscribe for invitations to events and classes. **www.slowschool.com.au**
CORPORATE SERVICES	Carolyn offers the following services for organisations on the purpose journey:

- Bulk book purchases
- Book customisation
- Keynote speaking
- Strategic 'purpose' advice and consulting
- The *Purpose Project* 5-Day Immersion Program
- The *Talk on Purpose* Public Speaking Program.

Enquire at **carolyntate.co**

OTHER BOOKS BY CAROLYN

CONSCIOUS MARKETING
How to create an awesome business with a new approach to marketing

Conscious Marketing teaches you how to bring a higher purpose to marketing your business that can benefit customers, employees, investors, suppliers and the community. Through innovative principles and in-depth case studies, this book shows you how to turn your business into a movement that people will want to join.

With over 30 years of experience in marketing and business, author Carolyn Tate presents a model that will show you how to:

▶ Define your company's purpose as the central force for all your marketing activities

▶ Build a community that is truly inspired to help you grow your business

▶ Create compelling products and services that your customers will want to buy

▶ Make your promotional activities less costly and more effective.

Drawing on the values from the 'slow' and 'conscious' business movements, *Conscious Marketing* will help you build a business that can grow your bottom line and serve the community.

UNSTUCK IN PROVENCE
The courage to start over

At the age of 46, after years of single-motherhood and the unbearable feeling that life is going nowhere, Carolyn decides to get radically unstuck.

After selling her home, giving away most of her belongings, putting her flagging business on hold and ending a destructive love affair, she takes her 12-year-old son Billy to live in Aix-en-Provence, France.

Carolyn's very raw and real daily diary entries reveal how she goes about healing herself and recovering her spirituality, creativity and self-love. The pages also explore her, at times, tense but tender relationship with Billy, a boy on the cusp of becoming a teenager.

If you've ever needed the inspiration or courage to get unstuck – to shake off whatever it is in your life that's preventing you from being the woman you were destined to be – Unstuck in Provence is for you.